PRENTICE
THE AMERICAN NATION

Guided Reading and Review Workbook

PEARSON
Prentice Hall

Needham, Massachusetts
Upper Saddle River, New Jersey
Glenview, Illinois

ISBN 0-13-067871-6
16 17 18 19 20   10 09 08

Student Success Handbook..5

Unit 1 ★ Roots of American History

Chapter 1: Geography, History, and the Social Sciences (Prehistory–Present)
Section 1 17
Section 2 18
Section 3 19
Section 4 20

Chapter 2: Before the First Global Age (Prehistory–1600)
Section 1 21
Section 2 22
Section 3 23
Section 4 24

Chapter 3: Exploration and Colonization (1492–1675)
Section 1 25
Section 2 26
Section 3 27
Section 4 28
Section 5 29

Chapter 4: The Thirteen Colonies (1630–1750)
Section 1 30
Section 2 31
Section 3 32
Section 4 33
Section 5 34

Unit 2 ★ The Revolutionary Era

Chapter 5: Crisis in the Colonies (1745–1775)
Section 1 35
Section 2 36
Section 3 37

Chapter 6: The American Revolution (1775–1783)
Section 1 38
Section 2 39
Section 3 40
Section 4 41
Section 5 42

Chapter 7: Creating a Republic (1776–1790)
Section 1 43
Section 2 44
Section 3 45
Section 4 46

Chapter 8: Government, Citizenship, and the Constitution (1789–Present)
Section 1 47
Section 2 48
Section 3 49
Section 4 50
Section 5 51

Unit 3 ★ The Early Republic

Chapter 9: Launching the New Government (1789–1800)
Section 1 52
Section 2 53
Section 3 54
Section 4 55

Chapter 10: The Age of Jefferson (1801–1816)
Section 1 56
Section 2 57
Section 3 58
Section 4 59
Section 5 60

Chapter 11: The Nation Grows and Prospers (1790–1825)
Section 1 61

Section 2 62
Section 3 63
Section 4 64

Unit 4 ★ An Era of Expansion

Chapter 12: The Jacksonian Era (1824–1840)
Section 1 65
Section 2 66
Section 3 67
Chapter 13: Westward Expansion (1820–1860)
Section 1 68
Section 2 69
Section 3 70
Section 4 71
Section 5 72
Chapter 14: North and South (1820–1860)
Section 1 73
Section 2 74
Section 3 75
Section 4 76
Chapter 15: Reform and a New American Culture (1820–1860)
Section 1 77
Section 2 78
Section 3 79
Section 4 80

Unit 5 ★ Division and Reunion

Chapter 16: Slavery Divides the Nation (1820–1861)
Section 1 81
Section 2 82
Section 3 83
Section 4 84
Section 5 85
Chapter 17: The Civil War (1861–1865)
Section 1 86
Section 2 87
Section 3 88
Section 4 89
Section 5 90
Chapter 18: Reconstruction and the Changing South (1863–1896)
Section 1 91
Section 2 92
Section 3 93
Section 4 94

Unit 6 ★ Transforming The Nation

Chapter 19: The New West (1865–1914)
Section 1 95
Section 2 96
Section 3 97
Section 4 98
Section 5 99
Chapter 20: Industrial Growth (1865–1914)
Section 1 100
Section 2 101
Section 3 102
Section 4 103
Chapter 21: A New Urban Culture (1865–1914)
Section 1 104
Section 2 105
Section 3 106
Section 4 107

Unit 7 ★ New Role For The Nation

Chapter 22: The Progressive Era (1876–1920)
Section 1 108
Section 2 109
Section 3 110
Section 4 111
Section 5 112

Chapter 23: Becoming a World Power (1865–1916)
Section 1 113
Section 2 114
Section 3 115

Chapter 24: World War I (1914–1919)
Section 1 116
Section 2 117
Section 3 118
Section 4 119

Unit 8 ★ Prosperity, Depression, and War

Chapter 25: The Roaring Twenties (1919–1929)
Section 1 120
Section 2 121
Section 3 122
Section 4 123

Chapter 26: The Great Depression (1929–1941)
Section 1 124
Section 2 125
Section 3 126
Section 4 127

Chapter 27: The World War II Era
Section 1 128
Section 2 129
Section 3 130
Section 4 131
Section 5 132

Unit 9 ★ The Bold Experiment Continues

Chapter 28: The Cold War Era (1945–1991)
Section 1 133
Section 2 134
Section 3 135
Section 4 136
Section 5 137

Chapter 29: Prosperity, Rebellion, and Reform
Section 1 138
Section 2 139
Section 3 140
Section 4 141

Chapter 30: The Nation in a New World
Section 1 142
Section 2 143
Section 3 144
Section 4 145
Section 5 146

Epilogue
Section 1 147
Section 2 148
Section 3 149
Section 4 150
Section 5 151

Success in social studies comes from doing three things well—reading, testing, and writing. The following pages present strategies to help you read for meaning, understand test questions, and write well.

Reading for Meaning

Do you have trouble remembering what you read? Here are some tips from experts that will improve your ability to recall and understand what you read:

BEFORE YOU READ

Preview the text to identify important information.
Like watching the coming attractions at a movie theater, previewing the text helps you know what to expect. Study the questions and strategies below to learn how to preview what you read.

Ask yourself these questions:	Use these strategies to find the answers:
• What is the text about?	Read the headings, subheadings, and captions. Study the photos, maps, tables, or graphs.
• What do I already know about the topic?	Read the questions at the end of the text to see if you can answer any of them.
• What is the purpose of the text?	Turn the headings into *who, what, when, where, why,* or *how* questions. This will help you decide if the text compares things, tells a chain of events, or explains causes and effects.

AS YOU READ

Organize information in a way that helps you see meaningful connections or relationships.

Taking notes as you read will improve your understanding. Use graphic organizers like the ones below to record the information you read. Study these descriptions and examples to learn how to create each type of organizer.

Sequencing

A **flowchart** helps you see how one event led to another. It can also display the steps in a process.

Use a flowchart if the text—
- tells about a chain of events.
- explains a method of doing something.

TIP▶ List the events or steps in order.

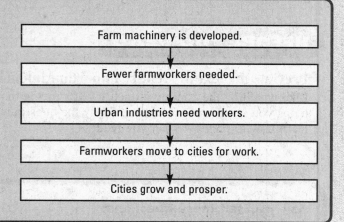

Farm machinery is developed.

Fewer farmworkers needed.

Urban industries need workers.

Farmworkers move to cities for work.

Cities grow and prosper.

Comparing and Contrasting

A **Venn diagram** displays similarities and differences.

Use a Venn diagram if the text—
- compares and contrasts two individuals, groups, places, things, or events.

TIP▶ Label the outside section of each circle and list differences.
Label the shared section and list similarities.

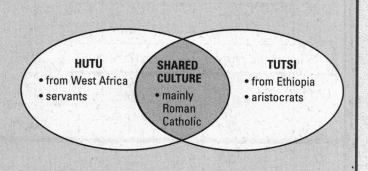

HUTU
- from West Africa
- servants

SHARED CULTURE
- mainly Roman Catholic

TUTSI
- from Ethiopia
- aristocrats

AS YOU READ

(continued)

Categorizing Information

A **chart** organizes information in categories.

Use a chart if the text—
• lists similar facts about several places or things.
• presents characteristics of different groups.

TIP▶ Write an appropriate heading for each column in the chart to identify its category.

COUNTRY	FORM OF GOVERNMENT	ECONOMY
Cuba	communist dictatorship	command economy
Puerto Rico	democracy	free enterprise system

Identifying Main Ideas and Details

A **concept web** helps you understand relationships among ideas.

Use a concept web if the text—
• provides examples to support a main idea.
• links several ideas to a main topic.

TIP▶ Write the main idea in the largest circle. Write details in smaller circles and draw lines to show relationships.

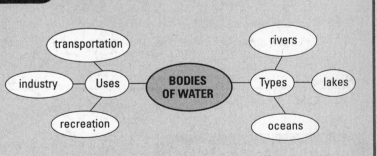

Organizing Information

An **outline** provides an overview, or a kind of blueprint for reading.

Use an outline to organize ideas—
- according to their importance.
- according to the order in which they are presented.

TIP▶ Use Roman numerals for main ideas, capital letters for secondary ideas, and Arabic numerals for supporting details.

> **I. Differences Between the North and the South**
>   **A.** Views on slavery
>   **1.** Northern abolitionists
>   **2.** Southern slave owners
>   **B.** Economies
>   **1.** Northern manufacturing
>   **2.** Southern agriculture

Identifying Cause and Effect

A **cause-and-effect** diagram shows the relationship between what happened (effect) and the reason why it happened (cause).

Use a cause-and-effect chart if the text—
- lists one or more causes for an event.
- lists one or more results of an event.

TIP▶ Label causes and effects. Draw arrows to indicate how ideas are related.

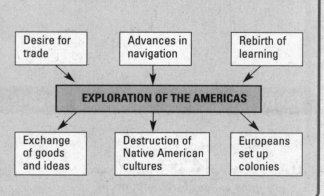

AFTER YOU READ

Test yourself to find out what you learned from reading the text.

Go back to the questions you asked yourself before you read the text. You should be able to give more complete answers to these questions:
- What is the text about?
- What is the purpose of the text?

You should also be able to make connections between the new information you learned from the text and what you already knew about the topic.

Study your graphic organizer. Use this information as the *answers*. Make up a meaningful *question* about each piece of information.

Taking Tests

Do you panic at the thought of taking a standardized test? Here are some tips that most test developers recommend to help you achieve good scores.

MULTIPLE-CHOICE QUESTIONS

Read each part of a multiple-choice question to make sure you understand what is being asked.

Many tests are made up of multiple-choice questions. Some multiple-choice items are **direct questions.** They are complete sentences followed by possible answers, called distractors.

Direct Question ➤	What is a narrow strip of land that has water on both sides and joins two larger bodies of land called?
The **distractors** list the possible answers. ➤	**A** a bay **B** an isthmus **C** a lake **D** an island
TIP▶ Try each distractor as an answer to your question. Rule out the ones that don't work. ➤	You can rule out A and C because they are bodies of water, not land. You can rule out D because an island is completely surrounded by water.

Other multiple-choice questions are **incomplete sentences** that you are to finish. They are followed by possible answers.

The **stem** tells you what the question is looking for ➤	A narrow strip of land that has water on both sides and joins two larger bodies of land is called
Distractors ➤	**A** a bay **B** an isthmus **C** a lake **D** an island
TIP▶ Turn the stem into a direct question, using *who, what, when, where,* or *why.* ➤	What is a narrow strip of land that has water on both sides and joins two larger bodies of land called?

WHAT'S BEING TESTED?

Identify the type of question you are being asked.

Social studies tests often ask questions that involve reading comprehension. Other questions may require you to gather or interpret information from a map, graph, or chart. The following strategies will help you answer different kinds of questions.

Reading Comprehension Questions

What to do:

How to do it:

1. Determine the content and organization of the selection.

Read the **title.** Skim the selection. Look for key words that indicate time, cause-and-effect, or comparison.

2. Analyze the questions.
Do they ask you to *recall facts?*

Look for **key words** in the stem:
According to the selection . . .
The selection states that . . .

Do they ask you to *make judgments?*

The main idea of the selection is . . .
The author would likely agree that . . .

3. Read the selection.

Read quickly. Keep the questions in mind.

4. Answer the questions.

Try out each distractor and choose the best answer. Refer back to the selection if necessary.

Example:

A Region of Diversity The Khmer empire was one of many kingdoms in Southeast Asia. Unlike the Khmer empire, however, the other kingdoms were small because Southeast Asia's mountains kept people protected and apart. People had little contact with those who lived outside their own valley.

Why were most kingdoms in Southeast Asia small?
A disease killed many people
B lack of food
C climate was too hot
D mountains kept people apart

TIP▶ The key word <u>because</u> tells why the kingdoms were small.
(The correct answer is D.)

WHAT'S BEING TESTED?

(continued)

Map Questions

What to do:	How to do it:
1. Determine what kind of information is presented on the map.	Read the map **title.** It will indicate the purpose of the map. Study the **map key.** It will explain the symbols used on the map. Look at the **scale.** It will help you calculate distance between places on the map.
2. Read the question. Determine which component on the map will help you find the answer.	Look for **key words** in the stem. About <u>how far</u> . . . [use the scale] <u>What crops</u> were grown in . . . [use the map key]
3. Look at the map and answer the question in your own words.	Do not read the distractors yet.
4. Choose the best answer.	Decide which distractor agrees with the answer you determined from the map.

Eastern Europe: Language Groups

In which of these countries are Thraco-Illyrian languages spoken?

A Romania
B Albania
C Hungary
D Lithuania

TIP▶ Read the labels and the key to understand the map.
(The correct answer is B.)

KEY
- ▢ Slavic languages
- ▢ Romance languages
- ▢ Thraco-Illyrian languages
- ▢ Baltic languages
- ▢ Non-Indo-European languages

Lambert Azimuthal Equal-Area Projection

Graph Questions

What to do:

1. Determine the purpose of the graph.

2. Determine what information on the graph will help you find the answer.

3. Choose the best answer.

How to do it:

Read the graph **title.** It indicates what the graph represents.

Read the **labels** on the graph or on the key. They tell the units of measurement used by the graph.

Decide which distractor agrees with the answer you determined from the graph.

Example

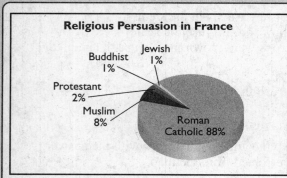

A **Circle graph** shows the relationship of parts to the whole in terms of percentages.

After Roman Catholics, the next largest religious population in France is

A Buddhist   **C** Jewish
B Protestant   **D** Muslim

TIP▶ Compare the percentages listed in the labels.
(The correct answer is D.)

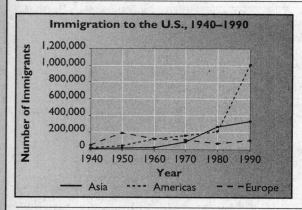

A **line graph** shows a pattern or change over time by the direction of the line.

Between 1980 and 1990, immigration to the U.S. from the Americas

A decreased a little   **C** stayed about the same
B increased greatly   **D** increased a little

TIP▶ Compare the vertical distance between the two correct points on the line graph.
(The correct answer is B.)

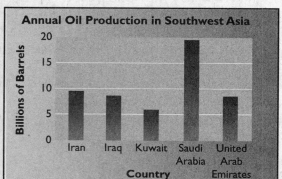

A **bar graph** compares differences in quantity by showing bars of different lengths.

Saudi Arabia produces about how many more billion of barrels of oil a year than Iran?

A 5 million   **C** 15 million
B 10 million   **D** 20 million

TIP▶ Compare the heights of the bars to find the difference.
(The correct answer is B.)

Writing for Social Studies

When you face a writing assignment, do you think, "How will I ever get through this?" Here are some tips to guide you through any writing project from start to finish.

THE WRITING PROCESS

Follow each step of the writing process to communicate effectively.

Step 1. Prewrite

- Establish the purpose.
- Define the topic.
- Determine the audience.
- Gather details.

Step 2. Draft

- Organize information logically in an outline or graphic organizer.
- Write an introduction, body, and conclusion.
- State main ideas clearly.
- Include relevant details to support your ideas.

Step 3. Revise

- Edit for clarity of ideas and elaboration.

Step 4. Proofread

- Correct any errors in spelling, grammar, and punctuation.

Step 5. Publish and Present

- Copy text neatly by hand, or use a typewriter or word processor.
- Illustrate as needed.
- Create a cover, if appropriate.

TYPES OF WRITING FOR SOCIAL STUDIES

Identify the purpose for your writing.

Each type of writing assignment has a specific purpose, and each purpose needs a different plan for development. The following descriptions and examples will help you identify the three purposes for social studies writing. The lists of steps will help you plan your writing.

Writing to Inform

Purpose: to present facts or ideas

Example

During the 1960s, research indicated the dangers of the insecticide DDT. It killed insects but also had long-term effects. When birds and fish ate poisoned insects, DDT built up in their fatty tissue. The poison also showed up in human beings who ate birds and fish contaminated by DDT.

TIP▶ Look for these **key terms** in the assignment: explain, describe, report, narrate

How to get started:
- Determine the topic you will write about.
- Write a topic sentence that tells the main idea.
- List all the ideas you can think of that are related to the topic.
- Arrange the ideas in logical order.

Writing to Persuade

Purpose: to influence someone

Example

Teaching computer skills in the classroom uses time that could be spent teaching students how to think for themselves or how to interact with others. Students who can reason well, express themselves clearly, and get along with other people will be better prepared for life than those who can use a computer.

TIP▶ Look for these **key terms** in the assignment: convince, argue, request

How to get started:
- Make sure you understand the problem or issue clearly.
- Determine your position.
- List evidence to support your arguments.
- Predict opposing views.
- List evidence you can use to overcome the opposing arguments.

Writing to Provide Historical Interpretations

Purpose: to present the perspective of someone in a different era

Example

The crossing took a week, but the steamship voyage was hard. We were cramped in steerage with hundreds of others. At last we saw the huge statue of the lady with the torch. In the reception center, my mother held my hand while the doctor examined me. Then, my father showed our papers to the official, and we collected our bags. I was scared as we headed off to find a home in our new country.

TIP▶ Look for these **key terms** in the assignment: go back in time, create, suppose that, if you were

How to get started:
- Study the events or issues of the time period you will write about.
- Consider how these events or issues might have affected different people at the time.
- Choose a person whose views you would like to present.
- Identify the thoughts and feelings this person might have experienced.

RESEARCH FOR WRITING

Follow each step of the writing process to communicate effectively.

After you have identified the purpose for your writing, you may need to do research. The following steps will help you plan, gather, organize, and present information.

Step 1. Ask Questions

Ask yourself questions to help guide your research.	What do I already know about the topic? What do I want to find out about the topic?

Step 2. Acquire Information

Locate and use appropriate sources of information about the topic.	Library Internet search Interviews
Take notes.	Follow accepted format for listing sources.

Step 3. Analyze Information

Evaluate the information you find.	Is it relevant to the topic? Is it up-to-date? Is it accurate? Is the writer an authority on the topic? Is there any bias?

Step 4. Use Information

Answer your research questions with the information you have found. (You may find that you need to do more research.)	Do I have all the information I need?
Organize your information into the main points you want to make. Identify supporting details.	Arrange ideas in outline form or in a graphic organizer.

Step 5. Communicate What You've Learned

Review the purpose for your writing and choose an appropriate way to present the information.	**Purpose**	**Presentation**
	inform	formal paper, documentary, multimedia
	persuade	essay, letter to the editor, speech
	interpret	journal, newspaper account, drama
Draft and revise your writing, and then evaluate it.	Use a rubric for self-evaluation.	

EVALUATING YOUR WRITING

Use the following rubric to help you evaluate your writing.

	Excellent	Good	Acceptable	Unacceptable
Purpose	Achieves purpose—to inform, persuade, or provide historical interpretation—very well	Informs, persuades, or provides historical interpretation reasonably well	Reader cannot easily tell if the purpose is to inform, persuade, or provide historical interpretation	Lacks purpose
Organization	Develops ideas in a very clear and logical way	Presents ideas in a reasonably well-organized way	Reader has difficulty following the organization	Lacks organization
Elaboration	Explains all ideas with facts and details	Explains most ideas with facts and details	Includes some supporting facts and details	Lacks supporting details
Use of Language	Uses excellent vocabulary and sentence structure with no errors in spelling, grammar, or punctuation	Uses good vocabulary and sentence structure with very few errors in spelling, grammar, or punctuation	Includes some errors in grammar, punctuation, and spelling	Includes many errors in grammar, punctuation, and spelling

Name _____ Class _____ Date _____

CHAPTER

1

Section 1 Guided Reading and Review
Thinking Geographically

A. As You Read

Directions: Complete the chart below as you read Section 1 in your textbook. Fill in details about the five themes of geography.

The Five Themes of Geography	
1. location	
2. place	
3. interaction	
4. movement	
5. regions	

B. Reviewing Key Terms

Directions: Explain how the following terms relate either to the five themes of geography or to maps and globes.

6. latitude _____

7. longitude _____

_____

8. natural resources _____

_____

9. cartographer _____

10. map projection _____

11. thematic map _____

CHAPTER

1

Section 2 Guided Reading and Review
Lands and Climates of the United States

A. Main Ideas

Directions: As you read Section 2 in your textbook, complete the chart with a brief description of each physical region or climate of the United States.

Physical Region	Climate
1. Pacific Coast	9. marine
2. Intermountain Region	10. Mediterranean
3. Rocky Mountains	11. highland
4. Interior Plains	12. desert/steppe
5. Appalachian Mountains	13. humid continental
6. Canadian Shield	14. tropical/humid subtropical
7. Coastal Plains	15. tundra/subarctic
8. Hawaiian Islands	

B. Reviewing Key Terms

Directions: Match the terms in Column I with the descriptions in Column II. Write the letter of the correct answer in the space provided.

Column I

_____ 16. isthmus

_____ 17. erosion

_____ 18. tributary

_____ 19. precipitation

_____ 20. altitude

Column II

a. rain, snow, sleet, or hail

b. height of the land above sea level

c. narrow strip of land

d. gradual wearing away of land

e. stream or river that flows into a larger river

Guided Reading and Review

CHAPTER

1

Section 3 Guided Reading and Review

The Tools of History

A. As You Read

Directions: As you read Section 3 in your textbook, correct each of the following false statements.

1. A secondary source is firsthand information about people or events.

   _____

2. A historian must first determine if a primary source is historic.

   _____

3. When evaluating authenticity, a historian must look for bias.

   _____

4. History is the study of evidence left by early people and civilizations.

   _____

5. Historians never study ordinary people who do the everyday things that shape the community.

   _____

6. Absolute chronology shows the time of an event in relation to other events.

   _____

B. Reviewing Key Terms

Directions: Define the following terms.

7. bias _____

   _____

8. artifact _____

   _____

   _____

9. archaeology _____

   _____

10. culture _____

    _____

11. chronology _____

    _____

Name _____ Class _____ Date _____

Section 4 Guided Reading and Review
Economics and Other Social Sciences

A. As You Read

Directions: As you read Section 4 in your textbook, complete the chart below by writing supporting details under each main idea.

Main Idea A: There are three basic economic questions each society must answer.

1. _____

2. _____

3. _____

Main Idea B: The American economic system is based on free enterprise.

4. _____

5. _____

Main Idea C: Other social sciences besides economics are important to the study of history.

6. _____

7. _____

8. _____

B. Reviewing Key Terms

Directions: Complete each sentence below by writing the correct term in the blank.

9. The study of how people manage their limited resources to satisfy their wants and

   needs is called _____.

10. A _____ is based on the exchange of money for goods and services.

11. _____ is the study of the rights and responsibilities of citizens.

12. The study of how peoples and cultures develop is called _____.

CHAPTER

2

Section 1 Guided Reading and Review

The First Civilizations of the Americas

A. As You Read

Directions: Complete the chart below as you read Section 1 in your textbook. Fill in details about each civilization.

1. Olmec	
2. Maya	
3. Aztec	
4. Inca	
5. Southwestern	
6. Mound Builders	

B. Reviewing Key Terms

Directions: Define the following terms.

7. surplus _____

8. quipu _____
_____

9. terrace _____
_____

10. pueblo _____
_____

© Pearson Education, Inc.

CHAPTER

2

Section 2 Guided Reading and Review
Native American Cultures

A. As You Read

Directions: As you read Section 2 in your textbook, cross out the term or name that does not belong in each group below. Then explain how the remaining terms are related.

1. driftwood   pit houses   seal oil   corn

_____

_____

2. potlatch   buffalo   canoes   villages

_____

_____

3. calendar   Natchez   igloo   Stinkard

_____

_____

4. adobe   tepees   buffalo   Great Plains

_____

_____

5. long house   confederacy   maple sugar   kachina

_____

_____

B. Reviewing Key Terms

Directions: Match the terms in Column I with the descriptions in Column II. Write the letter of the correct answer in the space provided.

Column I

_____ 6. tribe

_____ 7. pit house

_____ 8. kachina

_____ 9. clan

_____ 10. sachem

Column II

a. group of related families

b. community of people that share common customs, language, and rituals

c. house dug into the ground and covered with wood and skins

d. spirit represented by a masked dancer

e. Iroquois tribal leader

Guided Reading and Review

CHAPTER 2

Section 3 Guided Reading and Review

Trade Networks of Africa and Asia

A. As You Read

Directions: As you read Section 3 in your textbook, answer the following questions.

1. Why do the 1400s mark the beginning of the first global age? _____

   _____

2. Who founded Islam, and what do Muslims believe? _____

   _____

3. How was the growth of trade in the Middle East linked to the growth of Islam?

   _____

4. What were the major trade routes Muslim traders traveled? _____

   _____

5. What are some aspects of African village life? _____

   _____

6. Why did China not trade with outsiders until 1402? _____

   _____

B. Reviewing Key Terms

Directions: Complete each sentence below by writing the correct term in the blank.

7. Muslims practice a religion called _____, which was founded by the prophet Muhammad.

8. The _____ is the sacred book of Islam.

9. The _____ was an overland trade route that linked China and the Middle East.

10. _____ were groups of people who traveled together for safety.

11. A _____ is a large town whose government controls the surrounding countryside.

12. Several generations of an _____ live in one household.

Name _____ Class _____ Date _____

Section 4 Guided Reading and Review
Tradition and Change in Europe

A. As You Read

Directions: As you read Section 4 in your textbook, complete the chart below by writing supporting details under each main idea.

Main Idea A: Judaism and Christianity, two religions of the ancient Middle East, shaped European beliefs.

1. _____

2. _____

3. _____

Main Idea B: The customs of two ancient civilizations, Greece and Rome, shaped European traditions.

4. _____

5. _____

Main Idea C: The Middle Ages was a transition from the decline of the Roman empire to the modern era.

6. _____

7. _____

Main Idea D: The Renaissance expanded European geographical and intellectual horizons.

8. _____

9. _____

10. _____

B. Reviewing Key Terms

Directions: Define each term below, and identify the civilization or era with which it is associated: Jewish, Christian, Greek, Roman, Middle Ages, or Renaissance.

11. salvation _____

12. missionary _____

13. direct democracy _____

14. republic _____

15. feudalism _____

16. manor _____

17. Crusades _____

18. astrolabe _____

© Pearson Education, Inc.

CHAPTER

3 Section 1 Guided Reading and Review

An Era of Exploration

A. As You Read

Directions: Complete the chart below as you read Section 1 in your textbook. Fill in the missing causes and effects.

Causes	Effects
1.	Vikings left behind detailed records of their voyages.
Spain wanted a share of the Asian spice trade.	2.
Columbus returned to Spain with exotic gifts such as parrots and pearls.	3.
4.	Contact with the Europeans wiped out much of the Taino population of the West Indies.
5.	Europeans learned the true size of the Earth.
Europeans brought the first horses to North America.	6.

B. Reviewing Key People

Directions: Identify each of the following people. Include the country or region for which each sailed and the areas each explored, claimed, and/or settled.

7. Leif Ericson _____

_____

8. Christopher Columbus _____

_____

9. Vasco Núñez de Balboa _____

_____

10. Ferdinand Magellan _____

CHAPTER

3

Section 2 Guided Reading and Review

Spain Builds an Empire

A. As You Read

Directions: As you read Section 2 in your textbook, answer each of the following questions.

1. What motivated the Spanish conquistadors to sail to the Americas? _____

   _____

2. How were Cortés and Pizarro able to conquer the Aztecs and Incas? _____

   _____

   _____

3. What became of Álvar Núñez Cabeza de Vaca? _____

   _____

4. Why did Spaniards, such as De Soto and Coronado, fail to settle North America?

   _____

   _____

5. How did the king of Spain arrange for his new lands to be settled? _____

   _____

6. What were the four social classes in the Spanish colonies of North America?

   _____

   _____

7. Why did the Spaniards begin the Atlantic slave trade? _____

   _____

B. Reviewing Key Terms

Directions: Define the following terms.

8. conquistador _____

9. pueblo _____

10. presidio _____

11. mission _____

12. creole _____

13. mestizo _____

14. encomienda _____

CHAPTER

3

Section 3 Guided Reading and Review

Colonizing North America

A. As You Read

Directions: As you read Section 3 in your textbook, mark each statement true or false. Correct each false statement.

_____ 1. John Cabot and a crew of English sailors thought they had discovered the Northwest Passage. _____

_____ 2. Giovanni da Verrazano sailed up the St. Lawrence River on a voyage sponsored by France. _____

_____ 3. Henry Hudson explored the Hudson River for the Dutch and the Hudson Bay for the English. _____

_____ 4. Supporters of Queen Elizabeth I are called Protestants.
_____

_____ 5. French explorer Jacques Cartier founded Port Royal and Quebec in Canada.
_____

_____ 6. The French bought Manhattan Island from the local Indians.
_____

_____ 7. French and Dutch settlers in North America became rivals over the fur trade.
_____

B. Reviewing Key Terms

Directions: Use each term correctly in a sentence about the early French and Dutch settlement of North America.

8. Northwest Passage _____

_____

9. *coureur de bois* _____

_____

10. missionary _____

_____

11. alliance _____

_____

CHAPTER 3

Section 4 Guided Reading and Review

Building the Jamestown Colony

A. As You Read

Directions: As you read Section 4 in your textbook, complete each of the following sentences.

1. When Thomas Gates landed in Virginia in 1610, he found _____
_____

2. Walter Raleigh sent John White to Roanoke in order to _____
_____

3. The Virginia Company charter authorized _____
_____

4. Captain John Smith was an effective leader because he _____
_____

5. Jamestown began to prosper when the colonists _____
_____

6. The Virginia House of Burgesses was important because _____
_____

B. Reviewing Key Terms

Directions: Define the following terms.

7. charter _____
_____

8. burgess _____
_____

9. Magna Carta _____
_____

10. Parliament _____
_____

© Pearson Education, Inc.

CHAPTER

3

Section 5 Guided Reading and Review

Seeking Religious Freedom

A. As You Read

Directions: As you read Section 5 in your textbook, complete the chart below by writing supporting details for each main idea.

Main Idea A: It was not easy for people to practice religion freely in Europe during the 1500s.

1. _____
2. _____
3. _____

Main Idea B: Religious separatists decided to leave Europe and settle in North America.

4. _____
5. _____
6. _____

Main Idea C: The Pilgrims' first years in North America were difficult.

7. _____
8. _____

B. Reviewing Key Terms

Directions: Define the following terms.

9. established church _____

_____

10. persecution _____

_____

11. Mayflower Compact _____

_____

12. precedent _____

_____

© Pearson Education, Inc.

Name _____ Class _____ Date _____

Section 1 Guided Reading and Review
The New England Colonies

A. As You Read

Directions: As you read Section 1 in your textbook, complete the chart below. Fill in key similarities and differences among the New England colonies of Massachusetts Bay, Connecticut, and Rhode Island.

Similarities
1.
2.
3.
4.
5.
Differences
6.
7.
8.

B. Reviewing Key People

Directions: Identify each of the following people.

9. Charles I _____

10. John Winthrop _____

11. Thomas Hooker _____

12. Roger Williams _____

13. Anne Hutchinson _____

14. Metacom _____

© Pearson Education, Inc.

CHAPTER

4

Section 2 Guided Reading and Review
The Middle Colonies

A. As You Read

Directions: As you read Section 2 in your textbook, complete the chart below by writing supporting details for each main idea.

Main Idea A: The Dutch colony of New Netherland became the English colony of New York.

1. _____

2. _____

3. _____

Main Idea B: New Jersey attracted settlers from many lands.

4. _____

5. _____

Main Idea C: Pennsylvania was founded as an experiment in religious tolerance.

6. _____

7. _____

8. _____

B. Reviewing Key People and Terms

Directions: Identify each person or define each term below, and note whether it relates to New York, New Jersey, or Pennsylvania.

9. patroon _____

10. Peter Stuyvesant _____

11. proprietary colony _____

12. royal colony _____

13. Quaker _____

14. Pennsylvania Dutch _____

Name _____ Class _____ Date _____

Section 3 Guided Reading and Review
The Southern Colonies

A. As You Read

Directions: As you read Section 3 in your textbook, mark each statement true or false. Correct each false statement.

_____ 1. The Mason-Dixon Line marked the border between New England and the Middle Colonies. _____

_____ 2. Maryland was founded as a Catholic colony. _____

_____ 3. During Bacon's Rebellion, the city of Jamestown, Maryland, was burned. _____

_____ 4. Slavery quickly become common in North Carolina and South Carolina because of the rice plantations. _____

_____ 5. The first European settlers of Georgia were people who could not pay their debts. _____

_____ 6. Most of the great plantations in the South were located in the backcountry at the base of the Appalachians. _____

_____ 7. Many Africans who became slaves in the colonies were captured and sold into slavery by other Africans. _____

B. Reviewing Key Terms

Directions: Match the terms in Column I with the descriptions in Column II. Write the letter of the correct answer in the space provided.

Column I

_____ 8. Act of Toleration

_____ 9. indigo

_____ 10. debtor

_____ 11. slave code

_____ 12. racism

Column II

a. person who owes money

b. belief that one race is superior to another

c. law providing religious freedom to all Christians

d. plant used to make blue dye

e. laws that set out rules for slaves' behavior and denied their basic rights

CHAPTER

4

Section 4 Guided Reading and Review
Roots of Self-Government

A. As You Read

Directions: As you read Section 4 in your textbook, complete the chart below by writing supporting details under each main idea.

Main Idea A: England regulated trade with the North American colonies.

1. _____
2. _____
3. _____
4. _____

Main Idea B: Governments in all the colonies had certain characteristics in common.

5. _____
6. _____
7. _____

B. Reviewing Key Terms

Directions: Define the following terms.

8. mercantilism _____

_____

9. export _____

_____

10. triangular trade _____

_____

11. legislature _____

_____

12. bill of rights _____

_____

Name _____ Class _____ Date _____

CHAPTER

4

Section 5 Guided Reading and Review

Life in the Colonies

A. As You Read

Directions: As you read Section 5 in your textbook, complete the following sentences.

1. The gentry of colonial society included _____

   _____

2. Women in the colonies worked at many jobs, including _____

   _____

3. The Gullah language has its roots in _____

   _____

4. Two effects of the Great Awakening were _____

   _____

5. New Englanders believed in education for all children because _____

   _____

6. The basic belief of the Enlightenment era was _____

   _____

7. Benjamin Franklin's contributions to the city of Philadelphia included ____

   _____

8. The case of John Peter Zenger was important because _____

   _____

B. Reviewing Key Terms

Directions: Define the following terms.

9. middle class _____

   _____

10. indentured servant _____

    _____

11. apprentice _____

    _____

12. dame school _____

    _____

© Pearson Education, inc.

Guided Reading and Review

CHAPTER

5 Section 1 Guided Reading and Review

The French and Indian War

A. As You Read

Directions: Write the missing cause or effect as you read Section 1 in your textbook.

1. Cause: French trappers and traders in North America adopted Native American Ways.	1. Effect _____
2. Cause _____	2. Effect: Washington attacked the French but later surrendered.
3. Cause: General Braddock ignored warnings of Indian scouts near Fort Duquesne.	3. Effect _____
4. Cause _____	4. Effect: The best British generals were sent to North America.
5. Cause: The British won the Battle of Quebec.	5. Effect _____

B. Reviewing Key Places

Directions: Explain how each of the following places relates to the French and Indian War.

6. Ohio River _____

_____

7. Fort Duquesne _____

_____

8. Louisbourg _____

_____

9. Quebec _____

_____

CHAPTER

5

Section 2 Guided Reading and Review
Turmoil Over Taxation

A. As You Read

Directions: As you read Section 2 in your textbook, answer the following questions:

1. What was the cause of Pontiac's War? _____

   _____

2. What did the Proclamation of 1763 state? _____

   _____

3. How did colonists react to the Proclamation of 1763? Why? _____

   _____

4. Why did Parliament pass the Sugar Act? _____

   _____

5. What reason did the colonists have for protesting the Stamp Act? _____

   _____

6. What did the Townshend Acts create besides new taxes? _____

   _____

7. What activities did the Sons of Liberty and the Daughters of Liberty organize?

   _____

   _____

8. In what way did the Boston Massacre differ from earlier protests? _____

   _____

B. Reviewing Key People

Directions: Briefly identify each of the following people, and explain how each relates to the protests over taxes.

9. Samuel Adams _____

10. Mercy Otis Warren _____

11. Patrick Henry _____

12. Crispus Attucks _____

13. Paul Revere _____

© Pearson Education, Inc.

Name _____ Class _____ Date _____

CHAPTER

5

Section 3 Guided Reading and Review

From Protest to Revolution

A. As You Read

Directions: Each of the following statements is either true or false. As you read Section 3 in your textbook, mark each statement true or false. If a statement is false, correct the statement.

	True or False	**Correct Statement**
1. Sons of Liberty supported the tea boycott by throwing British tea overboard.		
2. The British passed the Intolerable Acts in response to the Boston Massacre.		
3. Other colonies could not agree whether or not to support Boston after the passage of the Intolerable Acts.		
4. The British marched on Concord to seize arms and ammunition.		
5. A professional colonial army opened fire on the British on Lexington Green.		

B. Reviewing Key Terms

Directions: Match the description in Column I with the terms in Column II. Write the letter of the correct answer in the space provided.

Column I

_____ 6. dumping of three shiploads of tea into Boston Harbor

_____ 7. meeting of representatives of all the colonies to decide on response to British policies

_____ 8. made lands between Ohio and Missouri Rivers part of Quebec

Column II

a. First Continental Congress

b. Quebec Act

c. Boston Tea Party

© Pearson Education, Inc.

Guided Reading and Review

Chapter 5 **37**

CHAPTER
6

Section 1 Guided Reading and Review
Fighting Begins in the North

A. As You Read

Directions: As you read Section 1 in your textbook, use the letters A–D to label the following events in correct chronological order. Write a sentence or two explaining the importance of each event.

_____ 1. the blockade of all colonial ports

_____

_____

_____ 2. the appointment of George Washington as Commander of the Continental Army

_____

_____

_____ 3. the Battle of Bunker Hill

_____

_____

_____ 4. the American victory at Fort Ticonderoga

_____

_____

B. Reviewing Key Terms

Directions: Complete the sentences in Column I with the terms in Column II. Write the letter of the correct term in the space provided.

Column I

_____ 5. The request of Congress that King George repeal the Intolerable Acts was called the _____.

_____ 6. The _____ was made up entirely of volunteers, most of whom had no military training or experience.

_____ 7. A/An _____ was a colonist who supported Britain.

_____ 8. When a/an _____ is set up, people and supplies cannot pass through a port.

Column II

a. Loyalist

b. Olive Branch Petition

c. blockade

d. Continental Army

© Pearson Education, Inc.

Name _____ Class _____ Date _____

Section 2 Guided Reading and Review
The Colonies Declare Independence

A. As You Read

Directions: As you read Section 2 in your textbook, complete the chart below by writing three supporting details under each main idea.

Main Idea A: Certain natural rights belong to all people from birth.

1. _____

2. _____

3. _____

Main Idea B: Great Britain committed many wrongs against the colonies.

4. _____

5. _____

6. _____

Main Idea C: The British colonies are now the United States of America.

7. _____

8. _____

9. _____

B. Reviewing Key Terms

Directions: Explain how each of the following relates to the American Revolution.

10. *Common Sense* _____

_____

_____

11. traitor _____

_____

_____

12. Declaration of Independence _____

_____

_____

CHAPTER 6

Section 3 Guided Reading and Review

Struggles in the Middle States

A. As You Read

Directions: As you read Section 3 in your textbook, answer the following questions:

1. What happened during the Battle of Long Island? _____
   _____

2. Who was Nathan Hale? _____
   _____

3. What was the result of the American attack on Trenton? _____
   _____

4. How did the Americans defeat Cornwallis at Princeton? _____
   _____

5. What was General Burgoyne's plan of attack? _____
   _____

6. Why was the British defeat at Saratoga important? _____
   _____

7. Name two Europeans who contributed to the American cause, and explain their
   contributions. _____
   _____
   _____

8. Describe conditions at Valley Forge in the winter of 1777–1778. _____
   _____

B. Reviewing Key Places and Terms

Directions: Identify each place, and define each term.

9. Battle of Long Island _____
10. Battle of Trenton _____
11. Battle of Saratoga _____
12. allies _____
13. cavalry _____
14. Valley Forge _____

© Pearson Education, Inc.

Name _____ Class _____ Date _____

6  Section 4 Guided Reading and Review

Fighting for Liberty on Many Fronts

A. As You Read

Directions: As you read Section 4 in your textbook, complete the chart below by writing key supporting details under each main idea.

Main Idea A: American women played important roles in the war.

1. _____

2. _____

Main Idea B: Many African Americans served in the war.

3. _____

4. _____

Main Idea C: Fierce battles were fought in the West.

5. _____

6. _____

Main Idea D: American ships struck some important blows for the Patriot cause.

7. _____

B. Reviewing Key People

Directions: Briefly identify the following people.

8. Mary Ludwig Hays _____
   _____

9. Peter Salem _____
   _____

10. Joseph Brant _____
    _____

11. George Rogers Clark _____
    _____

12. John Paul Jones _____
    _____

Name _____ Class _____ Date _____

6 Section 5 Guided Reading and Review
Winning the War in the South

A. As You Read

Directions: As you read Section 5 in your textbook, write the missing information under each heading.

Fighting in the South	Victory at Yorktown	The Peace Treaty
1. The British decided to try to win the war in the South because many _____ lived in the southern colonies.	5. General Cornwallis thought that if he conquered _____, he would cut off American supply routes to the South.	8. The Treaty of Paris stated that the _____ formed the western border of the United States.
2. The Americans' greater knowledge of _____ put the British at a disadvantage in the South.	6. _____ was a skilled American general, but his name became a synonym for "traitor" when he agreed to turn over West Point to the British.	
3. Two American generals who helped turn the tide in the southern battles were _____ and _____.	7. Retreating to Yorktown was a serious mistake for the British because Yorktown was on a/an _____, and they were trapped with no means of retreat.	
4. Francis Marion was called the _____ because of his surprise appearances, sudden attacks, and quick retreats.		

B. Reviewing Key Terms

Directions: Match the descriptions in Column I with the terms in Column II. Write the letter of the correct answer in the space provided.

Column I

_____ 9. army surrounds and blockades an enemy position

_____ 10. approve

_____ 11. hit-and-run tactics

Column II

a. guerrilla

b. siege

c. ratify

Guided Reading and Review

© Pearson Education, Inc.

CHAPTER

7

Section 1 Guided Reading and Review

A Loose Confederation

A. As You Read

Directions: Complete the following sentences as you read Section 1 in your textbook.

1. Each state's constitution sets out _____

    _____

2. In 1777, the Continental Congress approved _____

3. Compared with the states, under the Articles Congress had _____

    _____

4. Maryland demanded that other states cede their claims to western lands because

    _____

5. Disputes continued to arise among states because _____

    _____

6. Without the power to tax, Congress _____

7. Britain refused to withdraw its troops from the Ohio Valley, and Spain

    _____

8. Under the Land Ordinance of 1785, the Northwest Territory would be

    _____

9. The Northwest Ordinance allowed a territory to request statehood if

    _____

10. Many Americans saw Shays' Rebellion as _____

    _____

B. Reviewing Key Terms

Directions: Complete each sentence by writing the correct term in the blank.

11. _____ is a list of freedoms that the government promises to protect.

12. The _____ set up a loose alliance of the 13 states.

13. The _____ set up rules for settling the Northwest Territory.

14. The _____ set up a government for the Northwest Territory.

15. In an uprising known as _____, farmers attacked the Massachusetts government for raising taxes.

CHAPTER

7

Section 2 Guided Reading and Review
The Constitutional Convention

A. As You Read

Directions: As you read Section 2 in your textbook, answer the following questions:

1. What was the original goal of the Constitutional Convention? _____
_____

2. Why is James Madison called "the Father of the Constitution"? _____
_____

3. Why did the delegates keep their debates secret? _____
_____

4. How would the legislature differ under the Virginia Plan and the New Jersey Plan?
_____
_____

5. What was Roger Sherman's main contribution to the Convention? _____
_____
_____

6. How was the dispute between states over the question of the slave population resolved?
_____
_____

7. What were the Northern and Southern positions on outlawing the slave trade?
_____
_____

8. How was this disagreement resolved? _____
_____

9. How would the Constitution be approved and go into effect? _____
_____

B. Reviewing Key Terms

Directions: Briefly describe the responsibilities of each branch of government.

10. legislative branch _____

11. executive branch _____

12. judicial branch _____

© Pearson Education, Inc.

Guided Reading and Review

CHAPTER

7

Section 3 Guided Reading and Review

Ideas Behind the Constitution

A. As You Read

Directions: As you read Section 3 in your textbook, fill in the graphic organizer with the ideas that influenced the Constitution of the United States.

The Roman Republic	The American Experience
1. _____	6. _____
2. _____	7. _____
Great Britain	**The Enlightenment**
3. _____	8. _____
4. _____	9. _____
5. _____	10. _____

B. Reviewing Key Terms

Directions: Define the following terms.

11. republic _____

12. dictatorship _____

13. Magna Carta _____

14. habeas corpus _____

CHAPTER

7

Section 4 Guided Reading and Review
Ratification and the Bill of Rights

A. As You Read

Directions: Complete the crossword puzzle below as you read Section 4 in your textbook.

Across

1. To approve the Constitution

4. Needed to protect basic liberties

5. Amendment that protects freedom of religion, speech, and the press

7. Assembly that proposed the first 10 amendments

Down

2. Believed in a strong national government

3. Last state to approve the Constitution

6. What Antifederalists thought states would be

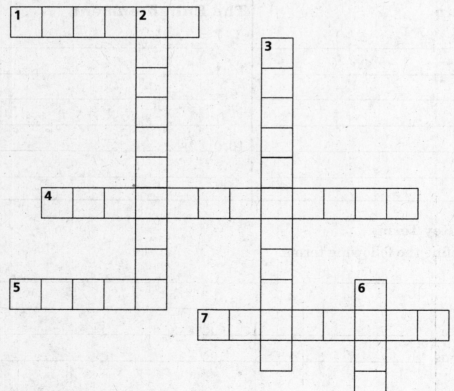

© Pearson Education, Inc.

B. Reviewing Key Terms

Directions: Define the following terms.

8. *The Federalist Papers* _____

9. amend _____

CHAPTER

8

Section 1 Guided Reading and Review

Goals and Principles of the Constitution

A. As You Read

Directions: As you read Section 1 in your textbook, complete the graphic organizer by writing in the goals and principles of the Constitution.

The Constitution

Goals

1.

2.

3.

4.

5.

6.

Principles

7.

8.

9.

10.

11.

12.

13.

B. Reviewing Key Terms

Directions: Define the following terms.

14. Preamble _____

15. Articles _____

16. general welfare _____

Name _____ Class _____ Date _____

Section 2 Guided Reading and Review

How the Federal Government Works

A. As You Read

Directions: As you read Section 2 in your textbook, complete the chart below by listing key facts that describe each branch of government.

	Legislative	Executive	Judicial (Supreme Court)
Officer(s)	1. 2.	8. 9.	12.
Primary Duty	3.	10.	13.
Checks on other branches	4. 5. 6. 7.	11.	14.

B. Reviewing Key Terms

Directions: Define the following terms.

15. bill _____

16. electoral college _____

17. appeal _____

18. veto _____

19. override _____

20. impeach _____

CHAPTER

8 Section 3 Guided Reading and Review

Changing the Constitution

A. As You Read

Directions: As you read Section 3 in your textbook, answer the following questions:

1. Why did the framers provide for changes to the Constitution? _____

_____

2. What are the two ways in which an amendment to the Constitution can be ratified? _____

_____

_____

3. What is the overall purpose of the Bill of Rights? _____

_____

List the provisions of each of the 10 amendments in the Bill of Rights.

4. First: _____

5. Second: _____

6. Third: _____

7. Fourth: _____

8. Fifth: _____

9. Sixth: _____

10. Seventh: _____

11. Eighth: _____

12. Ninth: _____

13. Tenth: _____

B. Reviewing Key Terms

Directions: Explain what each of the following added to the Constitution.

14. Civil War Amendments _____

_____

15. Nineteenth Amendment _____

_____

16. Twenty-sixth Amendment _____

_____

© Pearson Education, Inc.

Name _____ Class _____ Date _____

Section 4 Guided Reading and Review

State and Local Governments

A. As You Read

Directions: As you read Section 4 in your textbook, complete the graphic organizer by listing the powers and services of state and local governments.

State Governments	Local Governments
Power determined by: 1. _____ Services 2. _____ 3. _____ 4. _____ 5. _____ 6. _____ 7. _____ 8. _____ 9. _____ 10. _____	Power Determined by: 11. _____ Services 12. _____ 13. _____ 14. _____ 15. _____ 16. _____

B. Reviewing Key Terms

Directions: Define the following terms.

17. constitutional initiative _____

18. infrastructure _____

19. local government _____

Name _____ Class _____ Date _____

Section 5 Guided Reading and Review
Rights and Responsibilities of Citizens

A. As You Read

Directions: As you read Section 5 in your textbook, answer the following questions:

1. In what two ways can a person be considered a citizen of the United States by birth?

_____

_____

2. How does an adult become a naturalized citizen? _____

_____

3. What are some basic rights United States citizens enjoy? _____

_____

List six basic responsibilities of a citizen, and give one reason for fulfilling each.

4. _____

5. _____

6. _____

7. _____

8. _____

9. _____

B. Reviewing Key Terms

Directions: Complete the sentences in Column I with the terms in Column II. Write the letter of the correct answer in the space provided.

Column I

_____ 10. A feeling of love and devotion toward one's country is called _____.

_____ 11. A/An _____ is a person who enters another country in order to settle there.

_____ 12. A/An _____ is a noncitizen living in the country.

_____ 13. Every citizen has a responsibility to serve when called for _____.

_____ 14. A/An _____ citizen is one who has completed the official legal process for becoming a citizen.

Column II

a. jury duty

b. immigrant

c. naturalized

d. patriotism

e. resident alien

CHAPTER

9

Section 1 Guided Reading and Review

Washington Takes Office

A. As You Read

Directions: As you read Section 1 in your textbook, answer the following questions.

1. What were the first five executive departments of the federal government? _____
_____
_____

2. Who are members of the President's Cabinet, and what is their function? _____
_____

3. What did the Judiciary Act establish? _____
_____

4. How did Hamilton propose to repay the national debt, and what was the response of
the opposition? _____
_____

5. What steps did the government take to strengthen the economy? _____
_____

6. What was the purpose of the tax on whiskey? _____
_____

7. Who rebelled during the Whiskey Rebellion, and what was the outcome? _____

B. Reviewing Key People

Directions: Match each description in Column I with the correct name in Column II.
Write the letter of the answer in the space provided.

Column I

_____ 8. first President of the United States; served
two terms

_____ 9. first Secretary of State

_____ 10. first Secretary of the Treasury; set up the
Bank of the United States

_____ 11. led the opposition to the government's plan
for repaying the national debt

_____ 12. first Chief Justice of the Supreme Court

Column II

a. John Jay

b. Alexander Hamilton

c. George Washington

d. James Madison

e. Thomas Jefferson

© Pearson Education, Inc.

Guided Reading and Review

CHAPTER 9

Section 2 Guided Reading and Review

Creating a Foreign Policy

A. As You Read

Directions: As you read Section 2 in your textbook, complete the following sentences.

1. American responses to the French Revolution were _____
   _____

2. Washington's Cabinet members had the following opinions on the French
   Revolution: _____
   _____

3. The main foreign policy issue facing President Washington was _____
   _____

4. The Neutrality Proclamation stated that _____
   _____

5. Jay's Treaty provided that _____
   _____

6. In his Farewell Address, George Washington advised the nation _____
   _____

B. Reviewing Key Terms

Directions: Define the following terms.

7. French Revolution _____
   _____

8. foreign policy _____
   _____

9. neutral _____
   _____

10. Farewell Address _____
    _____

CHAPTER

9

Section 3 Guided Reading and Review

Political Parties Emerge

A. As You Read

Directions: Complete the chart below as you read Section 3 in your textbook. Fill in details about the differences between the Federalists and the Democratic Republicans.

	Federalists	**Democratic Republicans**
Basis of economy	1.	5.
Federal or state powers	2.	6.
Interpretation of the Constitution	3.	7.
Foreign policy	4.	8.

B. Reviewing Key People

Directions: Briefly identify the following people. Mark Federalists with an *F* and Democratic Republicans with a *DR*.

_____ 9. Alexander Hamilton _____

_____ 10. Thomas Jefferson _____

_____ 11. George Clinton _____

_____ 12. Aaron Burr _____

_____ 13. John Fenno _____

_____ 14. Philip Freneau _____

CHAPTER

9

Section 4 Guided Reading and Review

The Second President

A. As You Read

Directions: As you read Section 4 in your textbook, fill in supporting details for each of the main ideas listed below.

Main Idea A: As President Adams took office, the United States faced a crisis with France.

1. _____

2. _____

3. _____

Main Idea B: The Federalist Party split during the Adams administration.

4. _____

5. _____

Main Idea C: The Alien and Sedition acts raised the issue of states' rights.

6. _____

7. _____

8. _____

B. Reviewing Key Terms

Directions: Complete each sentence below by writing the correct term in the blank.

9. The _____ involved discussions between French agents and American diplomats.

10. President Adams did not want war, but he strengthened the navy by building

_____.

11. _____ is the act of stirring up rebellion against a government.

12. Kentucky and Virginia wanted to be able to _____ federal laws.

13. The _____ claimed that each state had the power to judge whether a law was unconstitutional.

CHAPTER 10

Section 1 Guided Reading and Review
A Republican Takes Office

A. As You Read

Directions: As you read Section 1, answer the following questions.

1. Why did Thomas Jefferson want to make the government more democratic?

_____

_____

2. How did Federalists feel about Jefferson's election?

_____

_____

3. What goals did Jefferson achieve in reducing the size of government?

_____

_____

_____

4. What action did Jefferson take when the Sedition Act expired?

_____

_____

5. What was the major difference in the philosophies of Jefferson and John Marshall?

_____

6. What was the outcome of *Marbury* v. *Madison*?

_____

_____

B. Reviewing Key Terms

Directions: Match the definitions in Column I with the terms in Column II.

Column I

_____ 7. idea that government should play as small a role as possible in economic affairs

_____ 8. an economy with little regulation

_____ 9. Supreme Court decides whether laws are constitutional

Column II

a. free market

b. judicial review

c. laissez faire

CHAPTER 10

Section 2 Guided Reading and Review
The Louisiana Purchase

A. As You Read

Directions: As you read Section 2, complete the following sentences.

1. Settlers west of the Appalachians relied on the Mississippi River for

_____

2. The United States wanted to purchase New Orleans and West Florida because

_____

_____

3. The French offered to sell all of Louisiana because

_____

4. Jefferson sent Lewis and Clark to explore the Louisiana territory because

_____

_____

_____

5. Sacagawea's contribution to the Lewis and Clark expedition was

_____

_____

6. The expedition had peaceful dealings with the Indians because

_____

7. Zebulon Pike explored

_____

_____

B. Reviewing Key Terms

Directions: Define each of the following terms.

8. Pinckney Treaty _____

_____

9. Louisiana Purchase _____

_____

10. continental divide _____

_____

Name _____ Class _____ Date _____

CHAPTER

10

Section 3 Guided Reading and Review

New Threats From Overseas

A. As You Read

Directions: As you read Section 3, complete the chart below by writing supporting details under each main idea.

Main Idea A: After the Revolution, American overseas trade grew rapidly.

1. _____

2. _____

3. _____

4. _____

Main Idea B: Britain and France violated American neutrality.

5. _____

6. _____

Main Idea C: Jefferson hoped that an American embargo would hurt Britain and
France.

7. _____

8. _____

9. _____

B. Reviewing Key Terms

Directions: Complete each sentence by writing the correct term in the blank.

10. To protect its ships from attack, the United States paid a _____ to
Tripoli.

11. British _____ gangs kidnapped young men and forced them into
service in the British navy.

12. A law banning trade is called an _____.

13. From 1807 to 1809, many American merchants violated trade laws by
_____.

Guided Reading and Review

Name _____ Class _____ Date _____

Section 4 Guided Reading and Review
The Road to War

A. As You Read

Directions: As you read Section 4, fill in the graphic organizer with the reasons why the United States and Britain went to war.

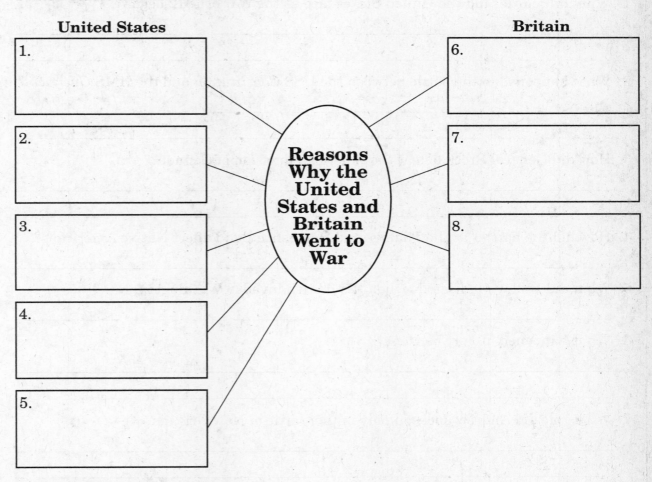

United States

1.

2.

3.

4.

5.

Reasons Why the United States and Britain Went to War

Britain

6.

7.

8.

B. Reviewing Key Terms

Directions: Identify each person listed below, and describe his role in the conflict between white settlers and Native Americans.

9. Tecumseh _____

_____

10. Tenskwatawa "The Prophet" _____

_____

11. William Henry Harrison _____

_____

CHAPTER 10

Section 5 Guided Reading and Review

The War of 1812

A. As You Read

Directions: As you read Section 5, answer the following questions.

1. What difficulties did the United States face as the War of 1812 began?

_____

_____

2. What happened in the battle between the USS *Constitution* and the HMS *Guerrière*?

_____

_____

3. How did General Brock defeat the American invasion of Canada?

_____

_____

4. How did the battles at the Thames and Horseshoe Bend affect Native Americans?

_____

5. What did Dolley Madison do when the British invaded Washington, D.C.?

_____

6. What happened at Fort McHenry?

_____

_____

7. What role did Andrew Jackson play in the Battle of New Orleans?

_____

_____

8. What did the United States and Britain agree to after the war ended?

_____

B. Reviewing Key Terms

Directions: Identify the significance of the following terms.

9. Battle of Lake Erie _____

10. Battle of New Orleans _____

11. Hartford Convention _____

12. Treaty of Ghent _____

CHAPTER

11

Section 1 Guided Reading and Review

The Industrial Revolution

A. As You Read

Directions: As you read Section 1 in your textbook, write one cause and one effect for each of the following events.

1. The Industrial Revolution began in Britain in the mid-1700s.

   Cause: _____

   Effect: _____

2. Samuel Slater memorized the design of the machines in British textile mills.

   Cause: _____

   Effect: _____

3. Eli Whitney invented machines that could manufacture identical parts.

   Cause: _____

   Effect: _____

4. Francis Cabot Lowell's partners built a factory town named for him.

   Cause: _____

   Effect: _____

5. Textile mills hired young women.

   Cause: _____

   Effect: _____

B. Reviewing Key Terms

Directions: Define the following terms.

6. spinning jenny _____

   _____

7. capitalist _____

   _____

8. factory system _____

   _____

9. urbanization _____

   _____

CHAPTER

11

Section 2 Guided Reading and Review
Americans Move Westward

A. As You Read

Directions: As you read Section 2 in your textbook, fill in the supporting details for each main idea.

> **Main Idea A:** Many settlers traveled westward during the early 1800s.
>
> 1. _____
>
> 2. _____
>
> 3. _____
>
> 4. _____
>
> **Main Idea B:** In the early 1800s, Americans found faster and better ways to travel or move goods by water.
>
> 5. _____
>
> 6. _____
>
> 7. _____

B. Reviewing Key Terms

Directions: Match the terms in Column I with the definitions in Column II. Write the letter of the correct answer in the space provided.

Column I

_____ 8. turnpike

_____ 9. corduroy road

_____ 10. *Clermont*

_____ 11. Erie Canal

Column II

a. road paved with logs

b. road on which tolls were collected

c. linked the Great Lakes with the Mohawk and Hudson rivers

d. began the age of steamboats

© Pearson Education, Inc.

CHAPTER

11 Section 3 Guided Reading and Review

Unity and Division

A. As You Read

Directions: Complete the chart below as you read Section 3 in your textbook. Fill in information to compare and contrast the ideas and political positions of three sectional leaders.

John C. Calhoun (South)	Daniel Webster (North)	Henry Clay (West)
1.	4.	7.
2.	5.	8.
3.	6.	9.

B. Reviewing Key Terms

Directions: Briefly define or identify each term.

10. Era of Good Feelings _____

_____

11. sectionalism _____

_____

12. American System _____

_____

13. internal improvements _____

_____

14. *McCulloch* v. *Maryland* _____

_____

15. *Gibbons* v. *Ogden* _____

_____

16. interstate commerce _____

_____

CHAPTER
11

Section 4 Guided Reading and Review
New Nations in the Americas

A. As You Read
Directions: Complete the following sentences as you read Section 4 in your textbook.

1. Latin American nations were eager for independence because _____
_____

2. Mexico gained its independence when _____
_____

3. The United Provinces of Central America included _____
_____

4. Latin American republics did not unite as a single country because _____
_____

5. Spain gave up its rights to Florida in exchange for _____
_____

6. The Monroe Doctrine stated that _____
_____

B. Reviewing Key People
Directions: Explain the role that each of the following people played in achieving Latin American independence.

7. Miguel Hidalgo _____
_____

8. José Morelos _____
_____

9. Simón Bolívar _____
_____

10. José de San Martín _____
_____

11. Prince Pedro of Portugal _____
_____

© Pearson Education, Inc.

Name _____ Class _____ Date _____

Section 1 Guided Reading and Review

A New Era in Politics

A. As You Read

Directions: As you read Section 1 in your textbook, fill in the chart to compare and contrast John Quincy Adams and Andrew Jackson.

	John Quincy Adams	**Andrew Jackson**
1. home state		
2. family background		
3. professional background		
4. political party		
5. political philosophy		

B. Reviewing Key Terms

Directions: Define each term.

6. suffrage _____

7. majority _____

8. Whig _____

9. Democrat _____

10. caucus _____

11. nominating convention _____

CHAPTER

12

![flag] **Section 2 Guided Reading and Review**

Jackson in the White House

A. As You Read

Directions: As you read Section 2 in your textbook, answer the following questions.

1. What was Andrew Jackson's early professional experience? _____

_____

_____

2. How did President Jackson plan to reform the government? _____

_____

_____

3. Why did Jackson oppose the existence of the National Bank? _____

_____

_____

4. What powers did the National Bank have? _____

_____

_____

5. How did Clay and Webster try to save the National Bank? _____

_____

_____

6. How did Jackson eventually destroy the National Bank? _____

_____

_____

B. Reviewing Key Terms

Directions: Use each term correctly in a sentence about the Jackson administration.

7. spoils system _____

_____

8. kitchen cabinet _____

_____

CHAPTER

12 Section 3 Guided Reading and Review

A New Crisis

A. As You Read

Directions: Complete the following sentences as you read Section 3 in your textbook.

1. Southerners hated the 1828 tariff because _____
_____
_____

2. Daniel Webster argued against nullification on the grounds that _____
_____
_____

3. The Indian Removal Act forced Indians to _____
_____
_____

4. Causes of the Panic of 1837 included _____
_____
_____

5. To ease the economic depression, President Van Buren _____
_____
_____

6. Changes in political campaigns that started in 1840 included _____
_____
_____

B. Reviewing Key Terms

Directions: Match each term in Column I with the correct definition in Column II. Write the letter of the correct answer in the space provided.

Column I

_____ 7. nullification

_____ 8. depression

_____ 9. mudslinging

Column II

a. a period in which business declines and many people lose their jobs

b. the use of insults to attack an opponent's reputation

c. cancellation

© Pearson Education, Inc.

Name _____ Class _____ Date _____

Section 1 Guided Reading and Review
Oregon Country

A. As You Read

Directions: As you read Section 1 in your textbook, write details about Oregon Country in the following chart.

Oregon Country	
Land	1.
	2.
	3.
Climate	4.
	5.
Journey to Oregon	6.
	7.
	8.
Who Traveled There	9.
	10.
	11.
	12.
Occupations in Oregon	13.
	14.
	15.

B. Reviewing Key People

Directions: Briefly identify each of the following people.

16. Jedediah Smith _____

17. Manuel Lisa _____

18. James Beckwourth _____

19. Marcus and Narcissa Whitman _____

_____

Name _____ Class _____ Date _____

Section 2 Guided Reading and Review
The Republic of Texas

A. As You Read

Directions: Use the letters A through E to put the following events into chronological order as you read Section 2 in your textbook. Write the letter in the space provided. Then, write a sentence about the importance of each event.

_____ 1. The Mexican army began the siege of the Alamo.

_____

_____

_____ 2. Mexico barred any more Americans from settling in Texas.

_____

_____

_____ 3. Sam Houston led his troops to victory at the Battle of San Jacinto.

_____

_____

_____ 4. The Republic of Texas declared its independence from Mexico.

_____

_____

_____ 5. Spain gave American Moses Austin permission to establish a colony in Texas.

_____

_____

B. Reviewing Key People and Terms

Directions: Complete the following sentences by writing the correct person or term in the space provided.

6. Mexicans who lived in Texas were called _____.

7. During the _____ no food or water could reach the Texans defending the Alamo.

8. The _____ resulted in the capture of General Santa Anna.

9. Texas was called the _____ Republic because of the design on its flag.

10. _____ became the first president of the Republic of Texas.

Name _____ Class _____ Date _____

CHAPTER

13 Section 3 Guided Reading and Review
California and the Southwest

A. As You Read

Directions: Below are three main ideas from Section 3 in your textbook. As you read, fill in the supporting details for each main idea.

Main Idea A: New Mexico Territory was home to three cultures.

1. _____

2. _____

3. _____

Main Idea B: Settlements in California included missions and ranches.

4. _____

5. _____

6. _____

7. _____

Main Idea C: Many Americans supported the idea of western expansion.

8. _____

9. _____

10. _____

B. Reviewing Key Terms

Directions: Briefly explain the relevance of each term to the westward expansion of the United States.

11. New Mexico Territory _____

12. Santa Fe Trail _____

13. Manifest Destiny _____

Guided Reading and Review

CHAPTER 13

Section 4 Guided Reading and Review

The Mexican War

A. As You Read

Directions: Write in the missing cause or effect as you read Section 4 in your textbook.

1. Cause: President Polk did not want to fight Britain for control of Oregon.	1. Effect: _____ _____
2. Cause: _____ _____	2. Effect: Congress admitted Texas to the Union.
3. Cause: Mexico refused to sell California and New Mexico to the United States.	3. Effect: _____ _____
4. Cause: _____ _____	4. Effect: Congress declared war on Mexico.
5. Cause: _____ _____	5. Effect: The Mexican government moved to make peace.
6. Cause: The United States needed a strip of Mexican land to complete a railroad.	6. Effect: _____ _____

B. Reviewing Key Terms

Directions: Match each term in Column I with the correct description in Column II. Write the letter of the correct answer in the space provided.

Column I	Column II
_____ 7. Bear Flag Republic	a. land in present-day Arizona and New Mexico that Mexico sold to the United States for $10 million
_____ 8. Treaty of Guadalupe-Hidalgo	b. stated that Mexico would cede California and New Mexico to the United States for $15 million
_____ 9. Mexican Cession	c. nickname given to California
_____ 10. Gadsden Purchase	d. lands Mexico sold to the United States at the end of the war

Name _____ Class _____ Date _____

13 Section 5 Guided Reading and Review
Americans Rush West

A. As You Read

Directions: As you read Section 5 in your textbook, answer the following questions.

1. Why did Joseph Smith and his followers move west? _____
_____
_____

2. Why did many Americans go to California? _____
_____
_____

3. Why were the people who joined the gold rush called "forty-niners"? _____
_____
_____

4. How did a miner get gold from the earth? _____
_____
_____

5. What effect did the gold rush have on California? _____
_____
_____

6. What did the gold rush mean for Mexican Americans and Indians? _____
_____
_____

B. Reviewing Key Places

Directions: Briefly explain the importance of the following places to westward expansion or the gold rush.

7. Salt Lake City _____
_____

8. Sutter's Mill _____
_____

9. San Francisco _____
_____

© Pearson Education, Inc.

72 Chapter 13   *Guided Reading and Review*

CHAPTER

14 Section 1 Guided Reading and Review

Industry in the North

A. As You Read

Directions: As you read Section 1 in your textbook, answer the following questions.

1. What could a sewing machine do that a tailor could not? _____
_____

2. How was John Deere's plow an improvement over earlier plows? _____
_____

3. What effect did Morse's telegraph have on American businesses? _____
_____

4. What were some of the problems with the first railroads? _____
_____

5. Why were clipper ships able to sail faster than other types of ships? _____
_____

6. What effects did factories, new machines, and railroads have on the northern economy in the mid-1800s? _____
_____

B. Reviewing Key Terms

Directions: Briefly explain the function of the following inventions.

7. reaper _____
_____

8. thresher _____
_____

9. telegraph _____
_____

10. locomotive _____
_____

11. clipper ship _____
_____

CHAPTER 14

Section 2 Guided Reading and Review

Life in the North

A. As You Read

Directions: Below are three main ideas from Section 2 in your textbook. As you read, fill in the supporting details for each main idea.

Main Idea A: Factory conditions in the North grew worse as the century advanced.

1. _____

2. _____

Main Idea B: Workers began organizing to improve conditions.

3. _____

4. _____

Main Idea C: Immigrants faced both opportunity and hardship in the United States in the 1840s.

5. _____

6. _____

7. _____

B. Reviewing Key Terms

Directions: Match each term in Column I with its definition in Column II. Write the letter of the correct answer in the space provided.

Column I

_____ 8. artisan

_____ 9. trade union

_____ 10. strike

_____ 11. famine

_____ 12. nativist

_____ 13. discrimination

Column II

a. severe food shortage

b. workers' refusal to do their jobs

c. one who wants to limit immigration and immigrants' rights

d. organized group of skilled workers who do the same types of jobs

e. policy or attitude that denies equal rights

f. skilled worker

© Pearson Education, Inc.

CHAPTER

14

Section 3 Guided Reading and Review

Cotton Kingdom in the South

A. As You Read

Directions: Write in the missing cause or effect as you read Section 4 in your textbook.

1. Cause: Eli Whitney invented a machine that could separate cotton seeds from fibers.	1. Effect: _____ _____
2. Cause: _____ _____	2. Effect: Slavery spread further throughout the South.
3. Cause: Conditions for growing cotton were limited to certain areas of the South.	3. Effect: _____ _____
4. Cause: _____ _____	4. Effect: Southern industry remained small-scale.
5. Cause: The South depended on the North for almost all of its manufactured goods.	5. Effect: _____ _____

B. Reviewing Key Terms

Directions: Define or identify each term.

6. cotton gin _____

7. Cotton Kingdom _____

CHAPTER 14

Section 4 Guided Reading and Review

Life in the South

A. As You Read

Directions: As you read Section 4 in your textbook, complete the following sentences.

1. Planters dominated southern society because _____

   _____

2. Slave owners created difficulties for free African Americans because _____

   _____

3. Rights that were denied to slaves included _____

   _____

4. African American families were often separated because _____

   _____

5. Christianity contributed to African American culture by _____

   _____

6. Slave revolts during the 1830s resulted in _____

   _____

B. Reviewing Key People and Terms

Directions: Define or identify the following people and terms.

7. cottonocracy _____

   _____

8. Denmark Vesey _____

   _____

9. slave codes _____

   _____

10. Nat Turner _____

   _____

Name _____ Class _____ Date _____

CHAPTER

15 Section 1 Guided Reading and Review

The Reforming Spirit

A. As You Read

Directions: As you read Section 1 in your textbook, fill in the chart below by writing in details of each reform movement.

hospital reform	1.
	2.
prison reform	3.
	4.
temperance movement	5.
	6.
education reform	7.
	8.
	9.

B. Reviewing Key Terms

Directions: Complete the following sentences by writing the correct term in the space provided.

10. In the mid-1800s, people became involved in _____ to improve unjust or imperfect conditions in society.

11. Many Protestants believed in _____, which held that God decided in advance which people would attain salvation after death.

12. A huge outdoor meeting intended to stir up or renew religious feeling is called a _____.

© Pearson Education, Inc.

Name _____ Class _____ Date _____

15  Section 2 Guided Reading and Review
Opposing Slavery

A. As You Read
Directions: Write in the missing cause or effect as you read Section 2 in your textbook.

1. Cause: In the 1800s, many Americans worked to end slavery.	1. Effect: _____ _____
2. Cause: _____ _____	2. Effect: A few thousand African Americans moved to Liberia.
3. Cause: Abolitionists formed the Underground Railroad.	3. Effect: _____ _____
4. Cause: _____ _____	4. Effect: Slave owners offered a $40,000 reward for the capture of Harriet Tubman.
5. Cause: _____ _____	5. Effect: Some northern manufacturers and workers opposed abolition.

B. Reviewing Key People
Directions: Briefly explain each person's contribution to the abolitionist movement.

6. Samuel Cornish _____

7. Maria Stewart _____

8. Frederick Douglass _____

9. William Lloyd Garrison _____

10. the Grimké sisters _____

11. Harriet Tubman _____

CHAPTER 15

Section 3 Guided Reading and Review

A Call for Women's Rights

A. As You Read

Directions: Answer the following questions as you read Section 3 in your textbook.

1. What rights did women lack in the mid-1800s?

   _____

   _____

2. Why was Sojourner Truth an effective leader in the fight for women's rights?

   _____

   _____

3. What was the purpose of the Seneca Falls Convention?

   _____

   _____

4. What educational opportunities did women have in the mid-1800s?

   _____

   _____

B. Reviewing Key People

Directions: Briefly explain the contributions of each person to the campaign for women's rights.

5. the Grimké sisters _____

6. Sojourner Truth _____

7. Lucretia Mott _____

8. Elizabeth Cady Stanton _____

9. Susan B. Anthony _____

10. Amelia Bloomer _____

11. Elizabeth Blackwell _____

CHAPTER

15

Section 4 Guided Reading and Review

American Art and Literature

A. As You Read

Directions: As you read Section 4 in your textbook, complete the chart below by writing in the names of important American artists and writers in each category. Briefly identify each person. One example is given.

painting	1.
	2.
	3.
poetry	4. Henry Wadsworth Longfellow, "Paul Revere's Ride" and "Hiawatha"
	5.
	6.
	7.
novels and stories	8.
	9.
	10.
	11.
	12.
	13.
	14.
philosophy	15.
	16.

B. Reviewing Key Terms

Directions: Define the following terms.

17. transcendentalists _____

18. civil disobedience _____

Guided Reading and Review

CHAPTER

16 Section 1 Guided Reading and Review

Slavery in the Territories

A. As You Read

As you read Section 1 in your textbook, fill in the missing causes and effects.

Causes	Effects
Missouri applied for statehood as a slave state.	1.
2.	Slavery was legal in the Louisiana Purchase south of the Missouri border.
Many northerners opposed the spread of slavery into the West.	3.
4.	People opposed to the spread of slavery founded the Free-Soil party.

B. Reviewing Key Terms

Explain the relevance of each term to the debate over slavery.

5. Missouri Compromise _____

_____

_____

6. Wilmot Proviso _____

_____

_____

7. popular sovereignty _____

_____

_____

8. Free-Soil party _____

_____

_____

CHAPTER

16

Section 2 Guided Reading and Review

The Compromise of 1850

A. As You Read

As you read Section 2 in your textbook, answer the following questions:

1. Why were southerners against California's admission to the Union as a free state?

_____

_____

2. Why did congressmen believe that Henry Clay could resolve the debate? _____

_____

3. What was Calhoun's position on slavery in the West? _____

_____

4. Why was Daniel Webster willing to agree to a fugitive slave law? _____

_____

5. What were the five provisions of the Compromise of 1850? _____

_____

_____

_____

_____

_____

6. What was the northern reaction to the passage of the Fugitive Slave Act? _____

_____

7. What effect did *Uncle Tom's Cabin* have on the nation? _____

_____

B. Reviewing Key Terms

Briefly explain each person's contribution to the controversy over slavery.

8. Henry Clay _____

9. John C. Calhoun _____

10. Daniel Webster _____

11. Stephen Douglas _____

12. Harriet Beecher Stowe _____

Name _____ Class _____ Date _____

A. As You Read

As you read Section 3 in your textbook, mark each statement true or false. Correct each false statement.

_____ 1. Henry Clay suggested that the people of Kansas and Nebraska decide for themselves whether their territories would allow slavery.

_____

_____ 2. Southerners argued that the Kansas-Nebraska Act would overturn the Missouri Compromise.

_____

_____ 3. Most people who moved to Kansas did so in search of cheap land.

_____

_____ 4. In 1855, Kansas ended up with two governments.

_____

_____ 5. A southern senator was severely beaten on the Senate floor for speaking out in favor of the Kansas legislature.

_____

_____ 6. The Supreme Court ruled that the Missouri Compromise was unconstitutional.

_____

B. Reviewing Key Terms

Write a sentence describing each person's role in the escalating battle over slavery.

7. Stephen Douglas _____

_____

8. John Brown _____

_____

9. Charles Sumner _____

_____

10. Dred Scott _____

_____

11. Frederick Douglass _____

_____

CHAPTER

16 Section 4 Guided Reading and Review

The Republican Party Emerges

A. As You Read

As you read Section 4 in your textbook, complete each sentence.

1. The main goal of the new Republican party was _____

2. The Republican candidate's popularity in the national election of 1856 made

    southerners _____

3. The Senate campaign between Lincoln and Douglas received national attention

    because _____

4. Before running for the Senate, Lincoln _____

5. At Harpers Ferry, John Brown _____

B. Reviewing Key Terms

Match each person with his description.

_____ 6. John C. Frémont

_____ 7. James Buchanan

_____ 8. Abraham Lincoln

_____ 9. Stephen Douglas

_____ 10. John Brown

a. first Republican candidate for President

b. Democrat who became President in 1856

c. Illinois senator who believed slavery question should be settled by popular sovereignty

d. Republican who ran for Illinois senate; gained national attention for his speeches against slavery

e. led what was planned to be a national slave uprising; tried for treason and executed

Name _____ Class _____ Date _____

CHAPTER

16 Section 5 Guided Reading and Review

A Nation Divides

A. As You Read

As you read Section 5 in your textbook, list supporting ideas for each main idea below:

Main Idea A: The national election of 1860 reflected sectional divisions.

1. _____

2. _____

3. _____

Main Idea B: The South reacted strongly to the election results.

4. _____

5. _____

6. _____

7. _____

B. Reviewing Key Terms

Briefly identify the importance of each place to the 1860 elections and/or the start of the Civil War.

8. Chicago, Illinois _____

9. South Carolina _____

10. Fort Sumter _____

© Pearson Education, Inc.

CHAPTER

17

Section 1 Guided Reading and Review

The Conflict Takes Shape

A. As You Read

As you read Section 1 in your textbook, use the graphic organizer to compare and contrast the two sides fighting in the Civil War.

	United States of America	Confederate States of America
1. President		
2. Number of states		
3. Reasons for fighting		
4. Position on states' rights		
5. Population		
6. Economy		
7. Army		
8. Military leaders		

B. Reviewing Key Terms

Briefly define each term.

9. border state _____

10. martial law _____

CHAPTER

17

Section 2 Guided Reading and Review

No Easy Victory

A. As You Read

As you read Section 2 in your textbook, answer the following questions.

1. What was the Union strategy for winning the war? _____
_____

2. Why did the Confederacy expect help from Europe? _____
_____

3. Where and how did General Stonewall Jackson get his nickname? _____
_____

4. What did both sides learn from the Battle of Bull Run? _____
_____

5. What kind of commander was General McClellan? _____
_____

6. What was the purpose of the Union blockade of southern ports? _____
_____

7. What was the United States Navy's contribution to the war? _____
_____

B. Reviewing Key Terms

Briefly describe each battle, including the location and the winner.

8. Bull Run _____
_____

9. Antietam _____
_____

10. Fredericksburg _____
_____

11. Chancellorsville _____
_____

12. Shiloh _____
_____

CHAPTER

17

Section 3 Guided Reading and Review

A Promise of Freedom

A. As You Read

As you read Section 3 in your textbook, complete the following sentences:

1. Lincoln approached the issue of emancipation cautiously because _____

_____

_____

2. The Emancipation Proclamation stated that _____

_____

_____

3. European reaction to the Emancipation Proclamation was _____

_____

_____

4. African Americans fought in the Union army because _____

_____

_____

5. The 54th Massachusetts Regiment is famous because _____

_____

_____

6. Slaves in the Confederacy responded to the Emancipation Proclamation by _____

_____

_____

B. Reviewing Key Terms

Briefly explain the relevance of each term to the Civil War.

7. Emancipation Proclamation _____

_____

8. 54th Massachusetts Regiment _____

_____

9. Fort Wagner _____

_____

CHAPTER

17

Section 4 Guided Reading and Review

Hardships of War

A. As You Read

As you read Section 4 in your textbook, fill in supporting details for each main idea listed below:

Main Idea A: Army life was like a nightmare.

1. _____

2. _____

Main Idea B: Both sides faced difficulties on the home front.

3. _____

4. _____

Main Idea C: The war affected the economy on both sides.

5. _____

6. _____

Main Idea D: Women on both sides played an active role in the war.

7. _____

B. Reviewing Key Terms

Match each term with its definition.

_____ 8. draft

_____ 9. Copperhead

_____ 10. inflation

_____ 11. profiteer

a. northerner who opposed using force to keep the South in the Union

b. military service requirement

c. rise in prices and decrease in the value of money

d. manufacturer who charged excessive prices for goods that the government needed for war

CHAPTER

17

Section 5 Guided Reading and Review

The War Ends

A. As You Read

As you read Section 5 in your textbook, mark each statement true or false. Correct each false statement.

_____ 1. Lincoln appointed Grant commander of the army because Grant was efficient and an effective leader.

_____

_____ 2. A great victory at Vicksburg turned the tide of war in the Confederacy's favor.

_____

_____ 3. Union control of the Mississippi cut the Confederacy in two.

_____

_____ 4. The Battle of Gettysburg was a decisive victory for Robert E. Lee.

_____

_____ 5. The South would continue to fight for a year after the Battle of Gettysburg.

_____

_____ 6. Only five thousand men died at the Battle of Gettysburg.

_____

_____ 7. Grant believed that total war against the southerners was the only way to win the war.

_____

_____ 8. Lee was forced to sign harsh and inhuman terms of surrender to the Union.

_____

B. Reviewing Key Terms

Fill in each blank with the correct term.

9. Lincoln's brief speech in honor of the war dead is known as the _____.

10. _____ was the last attack at Gettysburg, in which the Confederate soldiers were to cross open ground, climb a steep hill, and open fire on the enemy.

11. As part of the policy of _____ against the South, railroads and crops were destroyed and cities were burned to the ground.

12. Lee surrendered to Grant at _____.

Guided Reading and Review

CHAPTER 18

Section 1 Guided Reading and Review

Early Steps to Reunion

A. As You Read

As you read Section 1 in your textbook, answer the following questions:

1. Why was it harder for southerners than for northerners to adjust to peacetime?

_____

_____

2. What were Lincoln's intentions toward the South after the war ended? _____

_____

_____

3. (a) What was the main goal of the Freedmen's Bureau? (b) What services did it provide?

_____

_____

4. What effect did Lincoln's assassination have on the United States? _____

_____

_____

5. What did Andrew Johnson do when he became President? _____

_____

_____

B. Reviewing Key Terms

Match each description at the left with a term or name at the right.

_____ 6. rebuilding of the South after the Civil War		a. John Wilkes Booth
_____ 7. required majority of white men in former Confederate states to swear loyalty to the Union		b. Reconstruction
_____ 8. agency that aided former slaves		c. Freedmen's Bureau
_____ 9. actor who shot President Lincoln and died soon after while hiding from police		d. Thirteenth Amendment
_____ 10. abolished slavery throughout the United States		e. Wade-Davis Bill

CHAPTER 18

Section 2 Guided Reading and Review
Radical Reconstruction

A. As You Read

As you read Section 2 in your textbook, complete each sentence.

1. Southern legislatures' response to the Thirteenth Amendment was _____
_____

2. Republicans were outraged at the black codes and President Johnson because
_____
_____

3. Radical Republicans' two chief goals were _____
_____
_____

4. The Fourteenth Amendment stated that _____
_____

5. The 1866 elections resulted in _____
_____

6. The Reconstruction Act required that _____
_____
_____
_____

7. President Johnson was impeached because _____
_____

8. Republicans supported the Fifteenth Amendment because _____
_____
_____

B. Reviewing Key Terms

Briefly identify the following terms.

9. Radical Reconstruction _____
_____

10. black codes _____
_____

Guided Reading and Review

Name _____ Class _____ Date _____

A. As You Read

As you read Section 3 in your textbook, fill in the missing causes and effects.

Causes	Effects
1.	Many northerners came South after the war.
African Americans in the South went to the polls in large numbers.	2.
3.	Some southerners formed a terrorist group called the Ku Klux Klan.
Reconstruction governments spent a lot of money on railroads, school systems, and telegraph lines.	4.
5.	Most freedmen worked the land and remained poor.

B. Reviewing Key Terms

Match each term with its definition.

_____ 6. scalawag

_____ 7. carpetbagger

_____ 8. sharecropper

a. farmer who rented land and was given seeds, fertilizer, and tools in return for a share of the crop at harvest time

b. southern Democrat's derogatory nickname for southern Republican

c. northerner who went to the South after the war

© Pearson Education, Inc.

CHAPTER

18 Section 4 Guided Reading and Review

The End of Reconstruction

A. As You Read

As you read Section 4 in your textbook, fill in supporting details for each of the main ideas listed below.

Main Idea A: Reconstruction came to an end in the 1870s.

1. _____

2. _____

3. _____

Main Idea B: After Reconstruction ended, African Americans in the South began losing their rights.

4. _____

5. _____

Main Idea C: Industries flourished in the New South.

6. _____

7. _____

B. Reviewing Key Terms

Briefly explain the relevance of each of the following terms to the end of the Reconstruction era.

8. poll tax _____

_____

9. literacy test _____

_____

10. grandfather clause _____

_____

11. segregation _____

_____

12. *Plessy* v. *Ferguson* _____

_____

Name _____ Class _____ Date _____

Section 1 Guided Reading and Review
Indian Peoples of the Great Plains

A. As You Read

As you read Section 1 in your textbook, complete the graphic organizer by filling in supporting details for each main idea.

Main Idea A: Horses and buffalo played a central role in the culture of the Plains Indians.

1. _____
2. _____
3. _____
4. _____
5. _____

Main Idea B: Men's and women's activities and duties differed.

6. _____
7. _____
8. _____
9. _____
10. _____
11. _____

B. Reviewing Key Places

Match each term with its definition.

_____ 12. tepee   a. sled pulled by a dog or horse

_____ 13. travois   b. dried buffalo meat

_____ 14. corral   c. enclosure for livestock

_____ 15. jerky   d. tent made by stretching buffalo skins on tall poles

CHAPTER
19 Section 2 Guided Reading and Review
Mining and Railroading

A. As You Read

As you read Section 2 in your textbook, list one cause and one effect of each of the following events:

1. Miners began to leave boomtowns.

Cause: _____

Effect: _____

2. Few miners ever got rich.

Cause: _____

Effect: _____

3. Lawlessness and disorder often were characteristics of boomtowns.

Cause: _____

Effect: _____

4. Construction of a transcontinental railroad was completed in 1869.

Cause: _____

Effect: _____

B. Reviewing Key Terms

Briefly define each term.

5. lode _____

6. vigilante _____

7. transcontinental railroad _____

8. subsidy _____

CHAPTER

19

Section 3 Guided Reading and Review

The Cattle Kingdom

A. As You Read

As you read Section 3 in your textbook, describe each of the following in two or three sentences:

1. cowhand _____
   _____
   _____
   _____

2. cattle drive _____
   _____
   _____
   _____

3. cow town _____
   _____
   _____
   _____

B. Reviewing Key Terms

Fill in the blanks with the correct terms.

4. A _____ was a long journey of cattle from the Southwest to railroad lines in Kansas and Missouri.

5. A _____ was a skilled Mexican rider who herded cattle on Southwestern ranches.

6. A _____ is used to lasso cattle.

7. _____ protected a rider's legs from thorny plants.

8. A gunshot or clap of thunder could start a _____, in which cattle set off at a run.

9. A _____ was a town in which cattle were held until they could be shipped east.

CHAPTER
19
Section 4 Guided Reading and Review
Indian Peoples in Retreat

A. As You Read

As you read Section 4 in your textbook, answer the following questions:

1. What were the terms of the Fort Laramie Treaty? _____

_____

2. What happened at the Chivington Massacre? _____

_____

3. What happened to the buffalo of the Great Plains? _____

_____

4. What was the cause of the Sioux War of 1876? _____

_____

5. What happened at the Battle of Little Bighorn? _____

_____

6. What effect did the Ghost Dance have on non-Native Americans? _____

_____

7. What happened at Wounded Knee Creek? _____

_____

8. What was the intention of the Dawes Act? _____

_____

B. Reviewing Key Terms

Briefly identify each person listed below.

9. Sitting Bull _____

10. John Chivington _____

11. George Armstrong Custer _____

12. Chief Joseph _____

13. Geronimo _____

14. Susette La Flesche _____

15. Helen Hunt Jackson _____

© Pearson Education, Inc.

Name _____ Class _____ Date _____

A. As You Read

As you read Section 5 in your textbook, complete the following sentences:

1. To encourage people to settle the West, the government passed the
_____.

2. African American homesteaders called themselves the _____ after
a book of the Bible that described the Jewish flight from slavery in Egypt.

3. The first farmers to settle Oklahoma were called _____ because
they grabbed their land before the official date.

4. Dangers caused by the dry climate of the Plains included _____
_____

5. Women's duties on the Plains farms included _____
_____
_____

6. Farmers formed the National Grange and the Farmer's Alliance because _____
_____

7. The Populist party supported these ideas: _____
_____

B. Reviewing Key Terms

Briefly explain the relevance of each term to the settlement of the West.

8. sod house _____
_____

9. sodbuster _____
_____

10. cooperative _____
_____

11. wholesale _____
_____

CHAPTER

20 Section 1 Guided Reading and Review

Railroads Spur Industry

A. As You Read

As you read Section 1 in your textbook, explain the importance of each of the following developments in the national railroad on American society and on the economy.

1. In 1886, Southern railroads adopted the Northern gauge. _____

_____

2. George Westinghouse invented the air brake. _____

_____

3. Companies began buying up small rail lines. _____

_____

4. Many industries boomed because of the railroad. _____

_____

B. Reviewing Key Terms

Use each term correctly in an accurate statement about the growth of the railroad.

5. gauge _____

_____

6. network _____

_____

7. consolidate _____

_____

8. rebate _____

_____

9. pool _____

_____

© Pearson Education, Inc.

CHAPTER

20 Section 2 Guided Reading and Review

The Rise of Big Business

A. As You Read

As you read Section 2 in your textbook, fill in the missing causes and effects.

Causes	Effects
The Bessemer process allowed stronger steel to be produced more cheaply.	1.
2.	Carnegie had a great advantage over other steel producers.
J. P. Morgan invested in troubled corporations.	3.
Rockefeller knew that oil was not profitable until it was refined.	4.
5.	Corporations usually found ways to avoid regulations.

B. Reviewing Key Terms

Match each person with his description.

_____ 6. Henry Bessemer

_____ 7. Andrew Carnegie

_____ 8. J. P. Morgan

_____ 9. John D. Rockefeller

a. discovered a new way to convert iron into steel

b. Scottish immigrant to the United States who made a fortune in steel mills

c. built up his oil refineries into the Standard Oil Company of Ohio

d. banker who eventually gained control of U.S. Steel

© Pearson Education, Inc.

CHAPTER

20

Section 3 Guided Reading and Review

Inventions Change the Nation

A. As You Read

As you read Section 3 in your textbook, correct each of the following false statements:

1. The telephone was an instant success. _____

_____

2. Movies became possible with the invention of the light bulb. _____

_____

3. Assembly lines made it possible for people to eat fresh meat. _____

_____

4. Henry Ford charged less for his cars because he didn't care about making a profit.

_____

_____

5. The first airplane could fly 40 miles per hour and was used for wartime

   reconnaissance. _____

_____

B. Reviewing Key Terms

Identify the invention or inventions for which each of the following people is known.

6. Elisha Otis _____

7. Thomas Edison _____

8. Alexander Graham Bell _____

9. Lewis E. Waterman _____

10. King C. Gillette _____

11. George Pullman _____

CHAPTER

20

Section 4 Guided Reading and Review
The Rise of Organized Labor

A. As You Read
As you read Section 4 in your textbook, answer the following questions:

1. How did the relationship between worker and boss change after the Civil War?

_____

_____

2. What were the results of the 1885 strike at the Missouri Pacific Railroad?

_____

_____

3. What happened in Haymarket Square when workers clashed with strikebreakers?

_____

_____

_____

4. What were the goals of the American Federation of Labor?

_____

_____

5. What is Mother Jones best known for?

_____

6. Why is the Triangle Shirtwaist Company fire significant in the labor movement?

_____

_____

7. Why were unions not popular in the United States in the late 1800s?

_____

_____

B. Reviewing Key Terms
Complete each sentence below by writing the correct term in the blank.

8. A _____ is a workplace in which people labor long hours in poor conditions for low pay.

9. A _____ replaces a worker who has gone on strike.

10. _____ is the right of unions to negotiate with management on behalf of a group of workers.

11. The initials _____ stand for the famous union of garment workers that was founded in 1900.

CHAPTER

21 Section 1 Guided Reading and Review

New Immigrants in a Promised Land

A. As You Read

As you read Section 1 in your textbook, fill in the following chart with details about immigration in the late 1800s.

	Immigration
1. place of origin	
2. reasons for resettling	
3. journey to the United States	
4. life in the United States	
5. American response	

B. Reviewing Key Terms

Briefly identify each of the following terms.

6. pogrom _____

7. steerage _____

8. Statue of Liberty _____

9. acculturation _____

10. nativist _____

CHAPTER

21 Section 2 Guided Reading and Review

An Age of Cities

A. As You Read

As you read Section 2 in your textbook, mark each statement true or false. Correct each false statement.

_____ 1. By 1890, the majority of Americans lived in cities.

_____

_____ 2. Many African Americans migrated to northern cities to escape prejudice and find work.

_____

_____ 3. Many slum apartments had no windows, heating, or indoor bathrooms.

_____

_____ 4. The rich, the middle classes, and the urban poor all lived in the same neighborhoods.

_____

_____ 5. Unpleasant aspects of city life included garbage, pollution, and pickpockets.

_____

_____ 6. Religious organizations founded settlement houses to help the poor.

_____

_____ 7. Jane Addams is best known for helping to establish professional police and fire departments in Chicago.

_____

B. Reviewing Key Terms

Complete each sentence.

8. _____ meant that cities were becoming more and more crowded.

9. Only the poorest people in a city would live in a _____, with its lack of air, heat, and sanitation.

10. By the 1880s, _____ set standards for construction and safety of city housing.

11. The _____ spread the teachings of Christianity but also offered food and shelter to the poor.

12. The _____ helped preserve Jewish culture and provided community services.

CHAPTER

21

Section 3 Guided Reading and Review

Life in the Changing Cities

A. As You Read

As you read Section 3 in your textbook, complete the graphic organizer by filling in supporting details for each main idea.

Main Idea A: A building boom made remarkable changes to city life.

1. _____

2. _____

3. _____

Main Idea B: New diversions in cities made life there much more entertaining and fun.

4. _____

5. _____

6. _____

B. Reviewing Key Terms

Briefly define each term.

7. skyscraper _____

8. suburb _____

9. department store _____

10. vaudeville _____

11. ragtime _____

CHAPTER

21  Section 4 Guided Reading and Review

Public Education and American Culture

A. As You Read

As you read Section 4 in your textbook, fill in the missing causes and effects.

Causes	Effects
An industrial society needed educated workers.	1.
2.	The number of newspapers grew dramatically.
Girls as well as boys were sent to school and taught to read.	3.
4.	Realists wanted to show the costs of urbanization and industrial growth.
5.	Mark Twain's stories and novels were widely popular.

B. Reviewing Key Terms

Match each person with his or her description.

_____ 6. Joseph Pulitzer

_____ 7. William Randolph Hearst

_____ 8. Horatio Alger

_____ 9. Stephen Crane

_____ 10. Kate Chopin

_____ 11. Mark Twain

_____ 12. Winslow Homer

_____ 13. Thomas Eakins

_____ 14. Mary Cassatt

a. author of more than 100 rags-to-riches stories for children

b. moved to France and painted everyday scenes of mothers and children

c. writer of satirical stories and novels about serious issues

d. painter of medical and sporting scenes

e. publisher of the New York *World*

f. writer of stories about life in New Orleans

g. publisher of the New York *Journal*

h. painter of realistic scenes of New England coast

i. realist writer of *The Red Badge of Courage*

CHAPTER
22

Section 1 Guided Reading and Review
Reform in the Gilded Age

A. As You Read

Directions: As you read Section 1 in your textbook, answer the following questions:

1. What two concerns shaped politics in the Gilded Age? _____

_____

2. What did President Hayes do about corruption at the New York customhouse?

_____

_____

3. What did the Pendleton Act create? _____

_____

4. What did the Interstate Commerce Act of 1887 do? _____

_____

5. What were the results of the passage of the Sherman Antitrust Act? _____

_____

B. Reviewing Key Terms

Directions: Explain the relevance of each term to reform in the Gilded Age.

6. patronage _____

_____

7. merit _____

_____

8. civil service _____

_____

9. interstate commerce _____

_____

© Pearson Education, Inc.

CHAPTER

22 Section 2 Guided Reading and Review
The Progressives

A. As You Read
Directions: As you read Section 2 in your textbook, correct each false statement.

1. Political bosses fought corruption at all levels of government. _____

_____

2. Muckraking journalists ignored the need for reform. _____

_____

3. The Progressives were a unified political party. _____

_____

4. Robert La Follette's actions helped increase railroad rates. _____

_____

5. The Supreme Court decreed that after 1912, senators would be elected by the people
   instead of by legislatures. _____

_____

B. Reviewing Key Terms
Directions: Match each person with his or her description.

Column I

_____ 6. Thomas Nast

_____ 7. William Tweed

_____ 8. Jacob Riis

_____ 9. Ida Tarbell

_____ 10. Upton Sinclair

_____ 11. John Dewey

_____ 12. Robert La Follette

Column II

a. journalist and photographer who exposed slum conditions in New York

b. author of *The Jungle,* which exposed the meatpacking industry

c. Wisconsin governor who introduced reforms

d. corrupt political boss of New York City

e. journalist who exposed the Standard Oil Company

f. newspaper cartoonist who satirized corrupt politicians

g. Progressive educator

© Pearson Education, Inc.

CHAPTER

22

Section 3 Guided Reading and Review

Progressives in the White House

A. As You Read

Directions: As you read Section 3 in your textbook, compare and contrast the three Progressive Presidents by filling in details about each.

1. Theodore Roosevelt	
2. William Howard Taft	
3. Woodrow Wilson	

B. Reviewing Key Terms

Directions: Briefly identify each reform, specifying which President established each. Mark an R for Roosevelt, a T for Taft, or a W for Wilson.

_____ 4. Square Deal _____

_____ 5. Pure Food and Drug Act _____

_____ 6. New Freedom _____

_____ 7. Federal Reserve Act _____

_____ 8. Federal Trade Commission _____

Guided Reading and Review

CHAPTER

22 Section 4 Guided Reading and Review
Women Win Reforms

A. As You Read
Directions: As you read Section 4 in your textbook, complete each sentence.

1. The Seneca Falls Convention was the beginning of _____
_____

2. Western states granted women the right to vote because _____
_____

3. Carrie Chapman Catt helped the cause of suffrage by _____
_____

4. While picketing outside the White House, Alice Paul, Rose Winslow, and others
_____
_____

5. Women's clubs contributed to the fight for rights by _____
_____

6. Women supported the temperance drive because _____
_____

B. Reviewing Key Terms
Directions: Match each term or person with the correct description.

Column I	Column II
_____ 7. Carrie Chapman Catt	a. banned the sale of alcoholic drinks
_____ 8. suffragist	b. gave women the right to vote
_____ 9. Alice Paul	c. one who fought for women's right to vote
_____ 10. Nineteenth Amendment	d. radical temperance advocate
_____ 11. Carrie Nation	e. often arrested for her marches and protests in favor of suffrage for women
_____ 12. Eighteenth Amendment	f. organized a plan to fight for women's suffrage one state at a time

© Pearson Education, Inc.

CHAPTER 22

Section 5 Guided Reading and Review

Other Americans Seek Justice

A. As You Read

Directions: As you read Section 5 in your textbook, fill in the outline with details describing the experience of each ethnic group during the Progressive era.

Main Idea A: African Americans

1. _____

2. _____

3. _____

Main Idea B: Mexican Americans

4. _____

5. _____

6. _____

Main Idea C: Asian Americans

7. _____

8. _____

Main Idea D: Native Americans

9. _____

10. _____

B. Reviewing Key Terms

Directions: Briefly define or identify each term.

11. lynch _____

_____

12. NAACP _____

_____

13. barrio _____

_____

14. Gentleman's Agreement _____

_____

CHAPTER

23 Section 1 Guided Reading and Review

A Pacific Empire

A. As You Read

Directions: As you read Section 1 in your textbook, use the chart to compare and contrast the relationships between the United States and the nations listed.

1. Japan	
2. Russia	
3. Samoa	
4. Hawaii	
5. China	

B. Reviewing Key Terms

Directions: Use each term correctly in an accurate statement about the policy and actions of the United States in the Pacific.

6. isolationism _____

_____

7. expansionism _____

_____

8. annex _____

_____

9. imperialism _____

_____

10. sphere of influence _____

_____

CHAPTER

23 Section 2 Guided Reading and Review

War With Spain

A. As You Read

Directions: As you read Section 2 in your textbook, answer the following questions:

1. Why did President McKinley declare war on Spain? _____

_____

2. What was the cause of the Cuban rebellion of 1895? _____

_____

3. What was the reaction of the United States to the rebellion in Cuba? _____

_____

4. How did the newspapers of the day affect the situation? _____

_____

5. Why did the Americans fight in the Philippines? _____

_____

6. What was the outcome of the Spanish-American War? _____

_____

B. Reviewing Key Terms

Directions: Identify each person's role in the Spanish-American War.

7. William McKinley _____

8. José Martí _____

9. Joseph Pulitzer _____

10. William Randolph Hearst _____

11. Theodore Roosevelt _____

12. George Dewey _____

13. John J. Pershing _____

CHAPTER

23

Section 3 Guided Reading and Review

The United States in Latin America

A. As You Read

Directions: As you read Section 3 in your textbook, complete the following sentences:

1. President Roosevelt wanted to build a canal across Panama because _____

_____

2. The greatest obstacle to the workers digging the canal was _____

_____

3. Merchants and manufacturers benefited from the building of the Panama Canal because

_____

_____

4. Roosevelt extended the Monroe Doctrine to state that _____

_____

5. The United States wanted to keep Europe out of Latin America because _____

_____

6. The United States invested in Latin America because _____

_____

7. Relations between the United States and Mexico grew strained because _____

_____

B. Reviewing Key Terms

Directions: Match each term with its definition.

Column I	Column II
_____ 8. isthmus	a. policy of building strong economic ties between nations
_____ 9. corollary	b. addition
_____ 10. dollar diplomacy	c. strip of land connecting two larger bodies of land

CHAPTER 24

Section 1 Guided Reading and Review
War in Europe

A. As You Read

Directions: As you read Section 1 in your textbook, list one cause and one effect of each of the following events:

1. European nationalists demanded freedom and self-government.

   Cause: _____

   Effect: _____

2. The Archduke of Austria-Hungary and his wife were assassinated in Sarajevo in 1914.

   Cause: _____

   Effect: _____

3. Germany declared war on Russia and France.

   Cause: _____

   Effect: _____

4. Neither side gained much territory during four years of trench warfare.

   Cause: _____

   Effect: _____

5. The United States remained neutral for most of the war.

   Cause: _____

   Effect: _____

B. Reviewing Key Terms

Directions: Briefly define each term.

6. nationalism _____

7. militarism _____

8. terrorist _____

9. kaiser _____

10. stalemate _____

11. propaganda _____

© Pearson Education, Inc.

CHAPTER

24 Section 2 Guided Reading and Review

From Neutrality to War

A. As You Read

Directions: As you read Section 2 in your textbook, fill in supporting details for each main idea below:

Main Idea A: President Wilson tried to bring about peace.

1. _____

2. _____

Main Idea B: The United States began preparations to enter the war.

3. _____

4. _____

5. _____

6. _____

Main Idea C: Americans on the home front responded to the war effort.

7. _____

8. _____

9. _____

B. Reviewing Key Terms

Directions: Match each term with its definition.

Column I	Column II
_____ 10. warmonger	a. law requiring people of a certain age to serve in the military
_____ 11. czar	b. emperor of Russia
_____ 12. draft	c. unable to read or write
_____ 13. illiterate	d. person who tries to stir up war
_____ 14. bureaucracy	e. a system of managing government through departments run by appointed officials
_____ 15. pacifist	f. one who refuses to fight because of a belief that violence is wrong

CHAPTER 24

Section 3 Guided Reading and Review

Americans in Battle

A. As You Read

Directions: As you read Section 3 in your textbook, answer the following questions:

1. Why did Russia withdraw from the war? _____

_____

_____

2. What was the result of the Treaty of Brest-Litovsk? _____

_____

_____

3. What was the battle at Amiens like? _____

_____

_____

4. What did the United States Marines do at Belleau Wood? _____

_____

_____

5. What happened at the Battle of the Argonne Forest? _____

_____

_____

6. How did the war end? _____

_____

_____

7. What were the costs of the war? _____

_____

_____

B. Reviewing Key Terms

Directions: Briefly explain the importance of each place to the Great War.

8. Amiens _____

9. Belleau Wood _____

10. the Argonne Forest _____

CHAPTER

24 Section 4 Guided Reading and Review
The Failed Peace

A. As You Read
Directions: As you read Section 4 in your textbook, complete each sentence.

1. Wilson's goals after the war were _____

_____

_____

2. The purpose of the League of Nations was _____

_____

_____

3. The Treaty of Versailles stated that Germany must _____

_____

_____

_____

4. Americans reacted to the Versailles Treaty in the following way: _____

_____

_____

_____

5. The League of Nations failed because _____

_____

_____

B. Reviewing Key Terms
Directions: Briefly define each term below.

6. Fourteen Points _____

7. League of Nations _____

8. Peace of Paris _____

9. Big Four _____

10. Treaty of Versailles _____

© Pearson Education, Inc.

Name _____ Class _____ Date _____

Section 1 Guided Reading and Review
Politics and Prosperity

A. As You Read

Directions: As you read Section 1 in your textbook, answer the following questions:

1. Why did the Democrats lose the White House in 1920? _____

   _____

2. Why were the 1920 Cabinet members called the "Ohio Gang"? _____

   _____

3. What was the Teapot Dome scandal? _____

   _____

4. What were the domestic presidential policies in the 1920s? _____

   _____

5. What were the sources of the economic boom of the 1920s? _____

   _____

6. How were relations between the United States and Latin America characterized

   during this period? _____

   _____

7. What type of government was in place in the Soviet Union? _____

   _____

8. What happened at the Washington Conference of 1921? _____

   _____

B. Reviewing Key Terms

Directions: Identify each person listed.

9. Warren G. Harding _____

10. Andrew Mellon _____

11. Herbert Hoover _____

12. Albert Fall _____

13. Calvin Coolidge _____

14. Dwight Morrow _____

15. V. I. Lenin _____

16. Jane Addams _____

Guided Reading and Review

CHAPTER

25 Section 2 Guided Reading and Review

New Ways of Life

A. As You Read

Directions: As you read Section 2 in your textbook, complete the chart by describing the social changes in each category.

1. Prohibition	
2. Women's Rights	
3. Transportation	

B. Reviewing Key Terms

Directions: Use each term correctly in a sentence about the Roaring Twenties.

4. Prohibition _____

_____

5. bootleggers _____

_____

6. repeal _____

_____

7. League of Women Voters _____

_____

8. Equal Rights Amendment _____

_____

9. suburb _____

_____

CHAPTER

25 Section 3 Guided Reading and Review
The Roaring Twenties

A. As You Read

Directions: As you read Section 3 in your textbook, fill in the chart with examples of 1920s crazes, innovations, artists, and celebrities.

1. Dances	
2. Fashions	
3. Music	
4. Literature	
5. Celebrities	

B. Reviewing Key Terms

Directions: Match each person with his or her description.

Column I

_____ 6. Louis Armstrong

_____ 7. Bessie Smith

_____ 8. Ernest Hemingway

_____ 9. Sinclair Lewis

_____ 10. Eugene O'Neill

_____ 11. Langston Hughes

_____ 12. Zora Neale Hurston

_____ 13. Babe Ruth

_____ 14. Charles Lindbergh

Column II

a. hit 60 home runs in one season; record stood for over 30 years

b. flew solo across the Atlantic Ocean

c. playwright; wrote realistic dramas

d. writer and collector of African American folktales

e. poet; wrote "The Negro Speaks of Rivers"

f. trumpeter who helped create jazz music

g. jazz singer

h. author of *Babbit* and *Main Street*

i. author of *The Sun Also Rises* and *A Farewell to Arms*

Name _____ Class _____ Date _____

CHAPTER
25

Section 4 Guided Reading and Review
A Nation Divided

A. As You Read

Directions: As you read Section 4 in your textbook, fill in supporting details under each main idea below:

Main Idea A: Many Americans did not share in the boom of the 1920s.

1. _____

2. _____

3. _____

4. _____

Main Idea B: Communism's rise in the East made Americans fear a communist revolution in the West.

5. _____

6. _____

7. _____

B. Reviewing Key Terms

Directions: Briefly define each term.

8. company union _____

_____

9. sabotage _____

_____

10. anarchist _____

_____

11. deport _____

_____

12. nativism _____

_____

13. quota system _____

_____

© Pearson Education, Inc.

CHAPTER 26

Section 1 Guided Reading and Review
The Great Crash

A. As You Read

Directions: As you read Section 1 in your textbook, list one cause and one effect for each of the following:

1. Farmers' incomes fell during the 1920s.

   Cause: _____

   Effect: _____

2. The stock market crashed on October 29, 1929.

   Cause: _____

   Effect: _____

3. The banking system was weakened.

   Cause: _____

   Effect: _____

4. Factories cut back on production.

   Cause: _____

   Effect: _____

5. Most Americans blamed President Hoover for the Great Depression.

   Cause: _____

   Effect: _____

B. Reviewing Key Terms

Directions: Complete each sentence by writing the correct term in the blank.

6. Many investors could not repay loans from stocks purchased _____.

7. October 29, 1929, the date of the stock market crash, is called _____.

8. People or businesses unable to pay their debts are described as _____.

9. Groups of shacks in which homeless people lived during the depression were called _____ because people blamed the President for the depression.

10. In 1932, the _____ marched to Washington to demand immediate payment of money not due to be paid until 1945.

CHAPTER

26 Section 2 Guided Reading and Review

FDR and the New Deal

A. As You Read

Directions: As you read Section 2 in your textbook, complete the chart below by writing key steps the government took to achieve each main goal of the New Deal.

Goal A: to provide relief for the unemployed

1. _____

2. _____

Goal B: to plan the economic recovery

3. _____

4. _____

5. _____

6. _____

7. _____

Goal C: to prevent another depression

8. _____

9. _____

B. Reviewing Key Terms

Directions: Briefly describe each New Deal program, and mark each A, B, or C to identify which of the above goals it helped achieve.

10. Civilian Conservation Corps _____

_____

11. Works Progress Administration _____

_____

12. National Industrial Recovery Act _____

_____

13. Public Works Administration _____

_____

14. Agricultural Adjustment Act _____

_____

Name _____ Class _____ Date _____

Section 3 Guided Reading and Review
Response to the New Deal

A. As You Read
Directions: As you read Section 3 in your textbook, list three ways in which the New Deal changed the United States government. Then, fill in the chart with arguments for and against these changes.

1. _____

2. _____

3. _____

For	Against
4.	5.

B. Reviewing Key Terms
Directions: Briefly define each term.

6. pension _____

7. collective bargaining _____

8. sit-down strike _____

9. deficit spending _____

10. national debt _____

CHAPTER

26 Section 4 Guided Reading and Review

The Nation in Hard Times

A. As You Read

Directions: As you read Section 4 in your textbook, answer the following questions:

1. What caused the dust storms that swept the Great Plains during the 1930s?

_____

_____

2. Why did farmers from the Great Plains pack up and migrate to California?

_____

_____

3. How did Eleanor Roosevelt change the job of First Lady? _____

_____

4. What special struggles did ethnic minorities face during the depression? _____

_____

_____

5. What did movies contribute to society during the depression? _____

_____

_____

B. Reviewing Key Terms

Directions: Briefly identify each artist's contribution to the depression.

6. John Steinbeck _____

_____

7. Thomas Hart Benton _____

_____

8. Dorothea Lange _____

_____

9. Orson Welles _____

_____

© Pearson Education, Inc.

Name _____ Class _____ Date _____

Section 1 Guided Reading and Review

The Gathering Storm

A. As You Read

Directions: As you read Section 1 in your textbook, fill in the graphic organizer with details of each country's government on the eve of World War II.

Soviet Union	1.
Italy	2.
Germany	3.
Japan	4.

B. Reviewing Key Terms

Directions: Briefly define each term, and note which country or countries it is associated with: use S for the Soviet Union, I for Italy, G for Germany, or J for Japan.

5. totalitarian state _____
_____
_____

6. fascism _____
_____
_____

7. Nazis _____
_____
_____

8. concentration camp _____
_____
_____

CHAPTER

27

Section 2 Guided Reading and Review
World War II Begins

A. As You Read

Directions: As you read Section 2 in your textbook, number the events below in chronological order. List one effect of each event.

_____ 1. Japan bombs Pearl Harbor, Hawaii.

Effect: _____

_____ 2. Hitler and Stalin agree to divide Eastern Europe between their nations.

Effect: _____

_____ 3. The German army invades France.

Effect: _____

_____ 4. Germany invades and annexes Austria.

Effect: _____

_____ 5. Japan declares all-out war on China and begins bombing major cities.

Effect: _____

_____ 6. The United States Congress passes the Lend-Lease Act.

Effect: _____

B. Reviewing Key Terms

Directions: Briefly define or identify each term.

7. Munich Conference _____

8. appeasement _____

9. blitzkrieg _____

10. Axis _____

11. Allies _____

12. Atlantic Charter _____

Name _____ Class _____ Date _____

Section 3 Guided Reading and Review
Americans in Wartime

A. As You Read
Directions: As you read Section 3 in your textbook, answer the following questions:

1. What did women do in the armed forces during the war? _____
   _____

2. Why were American consumer goods rationed during the war? _____
   _____

3. Why did America's entrance into the war have the effect that it did on the economy?
   _____
   _____

4. What kinds of changes did the war bring for women on the home front? _____
   _____
   _____

5. What caused the race riots in American cities in the 1940s? _____
   _____

6. What was the African American experience in the military? _____
   _____

7. What happened to Japanese Americans during the war? _____
   _____

B. Reviewing Key Terms
Directions: Use each term correctly in a sentence about the homefront during World War II.

8. War Production Board _____

9. victory garden _____

10. Rosie the Riveter _____

11. "Double V" Campaign _____

12. Tuskegee Airmen _____

CHAPTER
27  Section 4 Guided Reading and Review
The Allies Turn the Tide

A. As You Read

Directions: As you read Section 4 in your textbook, list the main events that happened to each country between 1942 and 1945.

1. Soviet Union

_____

_____

_____

2. Japan

_____

_____

_____

3. United States

_____

_____

_____

_____

4. Germany

_____

_____

_____

_____

B. Reviewing Key Terms

Directions: Briefly define or identify each term.

5. Battle of Midway _____

6. Operation Overlord _____

7. D-Day _____

8. Battle of the Bulge _____

CHAPTER

27

Section 5 Guided Reading and Review

The End of the War

A. As You Read

Directions: As you read Section 5 in your textbook, fill in supporting details under each main idea.

Main Idea A: One goal of the United States was to regain the Philippines.

1. _____

2. _____

Main Idea B: A second goal of the United States was to invade Japan.

3. _____

Main Idea C: Japan surrendered in 1945.

4. _____

Main Idea D: World War II was the deadliest war in history.

5. _____

6. _____

7. _____

8. _____

B. Reviewing Key Terms

Directions: Fill in each blank with the correct term.

9. The Americans captured steppingstones to Japan in a strategy known as

_____.

10. A _____ pilot is one who uses his own plane as a missile, knowing that he will die when he hits his target.

11. The _____ warned Japan to surrender or face destruction.

12. The deliberate massacre of millions of Jews, Poles, Gypsies, and Slavs is known as

the _____.

13. At the _____, 12 Nazis were sentenced to death for war crimes, and thousands more were imprisoned.

CHAPTER

28 Section 1 Guided Reading and Review

The Cold War Begins

A. As You Read

Directions: As you read Section 1 in the textbook, list one cause and one effect of each of the following events:

1. After World War II, the Soviet Union's relationship with Britain and the United States was one of distrust.

   Cause: _____

   Effect: _____

2. President Truman decided on a Cold War policy of containment.

   Cause: _____

   Effect: _____

3. Secretary of State George Marshall urged passage of the Marshall Plan.

   Cause: _____

   Effect: _____

4. President Truman approved an airlift to West Berlin.

   Cause: _____

   Effect: _____

5. The East German government built the Berlin Wall.

   Cause: _____

   Effect: _____

B. Reviewing Key Terms

Directions: Complete each sentence by writing the correct term in the blank.

6. The _____ was an intense rivalry and standoff between the forces of communism and democracy.

7. After World War II, many eastern European countries became _____ of the Soviet Union.

8. The _____ was an imaginary barrier between communist nations and democratically governed countries.

9. The _____ set out a program encouraging nations to resist communist expansion.

10. The _____, an international peacekeeping force, was the successor to the failed League of Nations.

CHAPTER

28

Section 2 Guided Reading and Review
The Korean War Period

A. As You Read

Directions: As you read Section 2 in the textbook, answer the following questions:

1. What was the immediate cause of the Korean War? _____
_____

2. What was the UN response to the outbreak of fighting in Korea? _____
_____

3. What happened at Inchon? _____
_____

4. What role did China play in the Korean War? _____
_____

5. What was the source of the dispute between Truman and MacArthur? _____
_____
_____

6. What were the terms of the armistice between the two sides? _____
_____

7. What effect did the Korean War have on Americans at home? _____
_____

8. How and why did Joseph McCarthy become notorious? _____
_____

B. Reviewing Key Terms

Directions: Match each term with its definition.

Column I

_____ 9. 38th parallel

_____ 10. demilitarized zone

_____ 11. perjury

_____ 12. censure

Column II

a. officially condemn

b. lying under oath

c. line of latitude along which Korea was temporarily divided

d. an area with no military forces

Guided Reading and Review

CHAPTER

28

Section 3 Guided Reading and Review
Regional Conflicts

A. As You Read

Directions: As you read Section 3 in the textbook, describe the effects of the Cold War in each region or country.

1. Africa

   Effects: _____

   _____

   _____

   _____

2. Asia

   Effects: _____

   _____

   _____

   _____

3. Cuba

   Effects: _____

   _____

   _____

   _____

4. Latin America

   Effects: _____

   _____

   _____

   _____

B. Reviewing Key Terms

Directions: Briefly describe the purpose of each organization.

5. Alliance for Progress _____

6. Peace Corps _____

7. Organization of American States _____

8. National Aeronautics and Space Administration _____

CHAPTER

28

Section 4 Guided Reading and Review

The War in Vietnam

A. As You Read

Directions: As you read Section 4 in the textbook, answer the following questions:

1. What were the results of the peace conference after Ho Chi Minh defeated the French in Vietnam? _____
_____
_____

2. Who were the Vietcong? _____
_____
_____

3. Why did the United States become involved in Vietnam? _____
_____
_____

4. What did the Gulf of Tonkin Resolution state? _____
_____
_____

5. How did Americans at home feel about the Vietnam War? _____
_____
_____

6. Why was the Tet Offensive a turning point in the war? _____
_____
_____

7. What effect did the Vietnam War have in Cambodia? _____
_____
_____

B. Reviewing Key Terms

Directions: Briefly describe each person's role in the Vietnam War.

8. Ho Chi Minh _____

9. Lyndon Johnson _____

10. Richard Nixon _____

Guided Reading and Review

CHAPTER

28

Section 5 Guided Reading and Review

The Cold War Ends

A. As You Read

Directions: As you read Section 5 in the textbook, complete the following sentences:

1. Germans tore down _____ in 1989.

2. The United States had refused to recognize the Chinese communist government led by _____.

3. President Nixon became the first American President since the beginning of the Cold War to visit _____.

4. The Soviets and the Americans worked together on a policy of _____, which eased the tensions of foreign relations for both sides.

5. Soviet troops invaded _____ in 1979 in support of the communist government that had just seized power there.

6. _____ took office in 1981, firmly believing that the Soviet Union was the focus of evil in the modern world.

7. Soviet leader _____ instituted sweeping reforms to help his country solve its vast economic and social problems.

8. In Poland, labor leader _____ led the fight against the communists and later became the freely elected head of the government.

B. Reviewing Key Terms

Directions: Use each term correctly in a statement about the end of the Cold War.

9. SALT agreement _____

_____

10. Star Wars _____

_____

11. Solidarity _____

_____

12. glasnost _____

_____

© Pearson Education, Inc.

CHAPTER

29

Section 1 Guided Reading and Review
Postwar Politics and Prosperity

A. As You Read

Directions: As you read Section 1 in the textbook, give one cause and one effect for each statement.

1. During World War II, Congress passed the GI Bill of Rights.

   Cause: _____

   Effect: _____

2. President Truman was reelected in 1948.

   Cause: _____

   Effect: _____

3. In the 1940s and 1950s, the American population grew by many millions.

   Cause: _____

   Effect: _____

4. Suburban communities of identical houses and shopping malls became common.

   Cause: _____

   Effect: _____

5. The federal government built thousands of miles of highways.

   Cause: _____

   Effect: _____

6. Television became a major source of news and entertainment.

   Cause: _____

   Effect: _____

B. Reviewing Key Terms

Directions: Use each term correctly in an accurate statement about postwar America.

7. inflation _____

8. baby boom _____

9. standard of living _____

10. beatnik _____

© Pearson Education, Inc.

Guided Reading and Review

CHAPTER

29

Section 2 Guided Reading and Review

The Civil Rights Movement

A. As You Read

Directions: As you read Section 2 in the textbook, explain the importance of each of the following to the civil rights movement:

1. NAACP _____

_____

2. Brooklyn Dodgers _____

_____

3. *Brown* v. *Board of Education of Topeka* _____

_____

4. *Hernández* v. *Texas* _____

_____

5. Montgomery Improvement Association (MIA) _____

_____

6. Southern Christian Leadership Conference _____

_____

B. Reviewing Key Terms

Directions: Briefly define each term.

7. segregation _____

8. integration _____

9. civil rights movement _____

10. boycott _____

11. civil disobedience _____

© Pearson Education, Inc.

CHAPTER

29 Section 3 Guided Reading and Review

Protest, Reform, and Doubt

A. As You Read

Directions: As you read Section 3 in the textbook, correct each of the following false statements:

1. Americans were concerned that presidential candidate Richard Nixon might be more loyal to the Catholic Church than to the country. _____

_____

2. Lee Harvey Oswald became President after John F. Kennedy was assassinated.

_____

3. The Warren Commission ordered that Lee Harvey Oswald be executed for killing the President. _____

4. Lyndon B. Johnson's Great Society programs took money from the poor and gave it to the wealthy. _____

5. The counterculture movement arose as a result of protests against the Vietnam War.

_____

6. In the 1968 presidential election, Richard Nixon defeated Robert F. Kennedy.

_____

7. Nixon is best remembered for his economic policies. _____

_____

B. Reviewing Key Terms

Directions: Match each President with the description of his term of office.

Column I

_____ 8. John F. Kennedy

_____ 9. Lyndon B. Johnson

_____ 10. Richard M. Nixon

_____ 11. Gerald R. Ford

_____ 12. Jimmy Carter

Column II

a. high inflation; strong support for human rights

b. created Peace Corps; began space program; assassinated in third year of his term

c. covered up his connection to burglary of Democratic national headquarters; resigned presidency under threat of impeachment

d. pardon of Nixon lost him much public support

e. goal was for all Americans to achieve decent standard of living; created numerous social programs such as Head Start

CHAPTER

29 Section 4 Guided Reading and Review

The Crusade for Equal Rights

A. As You Read

Directions: As you read Section 4 in the textbook, identify and briefly describe the various methods people used to protest during the civil rights movement.

1.
2.
3.

B. Reviewing Key Terms

Directions: Briefly identify or describe the importance of each of the following:

4. Greensboro, North Carolina _____

5. Congress of Racial Equality _____

6. Voting Rights Act _____

7. Black Panthers _____

8. Malcolm X _____

9. Watts, Los Angeles, California _____

10. Thurgood Marshall _____

© Pearson Education, Inc.

CHAPTER

30 Section 1 Guided Reading and Review

The Conservative Revolt

A. As You Read

Directions: As you read Section 1 in the textbook, answer the following questions:

1. Why did the country become more conservative as the century ended? _____
_____

2. What were the goals of conservative citizens and politicians? _____
_____

3. Why was Ronald Reagan called "the Great Communicator"? _____
_____

4. What were Reagan's economic goals? _____
_____

5. What were the problems in George H.W. Bush's presidency? _____
_____

6. What were the successes in Bill Clinton's presidency? _____
_____

7. What was unusual about the 2000 presidential election? _____
_____

B. Reviewing Key Terms

Directions: Briefly identify or define each term.

8. Moral Majority _____
_____

9. Reaganomics _____
_____

10. deregulation _____
_____

11. Contract with America _____
_____

© Pearson Education, Inc.

CHAPTER

30 Section 2 Guided Reading and Review

American Leadership in a New World

A. As You Read

Directions: As you read Section 2 in the textbook, complete the following sentences:

1. The United States became the world's only superpower when _____

   _____

2. Filipino protest against dictator Marcos resulted in _____

   _____

3. China responded to a people's campaign for democratic reforms by _____

   _____

4. The United States and Russia continued to work together to _____

   _____

5. The Comprehensive Test Ban Treaty failed because _____

   _____

B. Reviewing Key Terms

Directions: Match each term with its definition.

Column I	Column II
_____ 6. apartheid	a. competition to have the most weapons
_____ 7. sanctions	b. strict separation of races
_____ 8. global democracy	c. establishment of freely elected governments all over the world
_____ 9. arms race	d. measures designed to make a country change its policies

CHAPTER

30 Section 3 Guided Reading and Review

The Spread of Regional Conflict

A. As You Read

Directions: As you read Section 3 in the textbook, fill in details about each regional conflict. For those conflicts not directly involving the United States, include a brief description of the role the United States has played in each conflict.

Arab-Israeli Conflict
1.
Iran and Iraq
2.
Terrorism and the United States
3.

© Pearson Education, Inc.

B. Reviewing Key Terms

Directions: Briefly identify each term. Note to which of the above conflicts it is most relevant.

4. OPEC _____

5. Camp David Accords _____

6. Palestinian Liberation Organization _____

7. Office of Homeland Security _____

CHAPTER
30

Section 4 Guided Reading and Review

A Global Economy

A. As You Read

Directions: As you read Section 4 in the textbook, fill in the missing causes and effects.

Causes	Effects
American companies pay workers higher wages than do companies in most other nations.	1.
2.	Trade boomed among Mexico, Canada, and the United States, and new jobs were created.
Environmental reformers called attention to the dangers of industrial waste and chemical pesticides.	3.
A scientist dreamed of a vast inter-connected network of computers.	4.

B. Reviewing Key Terms

Directions: Briefly define each term.

5. trade deficit _____

6. environmentalists _____

7. renewable resource _____

8. global warming _____

9. Internet _____

10. e-commerce _____

CHAPTER

30 Section 5 Guided Reading and Review

New Challenges for the Nation

A. As You Read

Directions: As you read Section 5 in the textbook, answer the following questions:

1. Why do so many Asians immigrate to the United States? _____

_____

_____

2. What is the function of the Immigration Reform and Control Act? _____

_____

_____

3. What is the current status of Native Americans? _____

_____

_____

4. What is the Americans with Disabilities Act? _____

_____

_____

5. Why has the population of the United States grown older? _____

_____

_____

6. What are two major challenges the United States faces in the twenty-first century?

_____

_____

B. Reviewing Key Terms

Directions: Briefly define each term.

7. refugee _____

8. illegal alien _____

9. mainstreaming _____

EPILOGUE

Section 1 Guided Reading and Review
Entering Modern Times

A. As You Read

Directions: As you read Section 1 in the textbook, answer the following questions:

1. What were some of the reasons people moved west after the Civil War? _____
   _____

2. What effect did the westward movement have on Native Americans? _____
   _____

3. What effect did technology have on American industry after the Civil War? _____
   _____

4. What was the relationship between banks and corporations? _____
   _____

5. What are the arguments for and against monopolies? _____
   _____

6. What was the importance of the American Federation of Labor? _____
   _____

7. What effect did immigrants have on American cities? _____
   _____

B. Reviewing Key Terms

Directions: Briefly identify each of the following people.

8. Thomas Edison _____

9. Andrew Carnegie _____

10. J. P. Morgan _____

11. John D. Rockefeller _____

Name _____ Class _____ Date _____

EPILOGUE

 # Section 2 Guided Reading and Review

A New Role for the Nation

A. As You Read

Directions: As you read Section 2 in the textbook, complete the following sentences:

1. The Progressive Era gets its name from _____

   _____

2. The Sixteenth Amendment was important because _____

   _____

3. Theodore Roosevelt's reforms included _____

   _____

4. United States foreign policy began changing because _____

   _____

5. Roosevelt's statement that the United States had a right to intervene in Latin American

   affairs became known as the _____

   _____

6. America declared war on Germany because _____

   _____

B. Reviewing Key Terms

Directions: Match each term with its definition.

Column I	Column II
_____ 7. muckraker	a. crusading journalist
_____ 8. isolationism	b. control of several countries by one country
_____ 9. imperialism	c. limited involvement in world affairs

Guided Reading and Review

EPILOGUE
 # Section 3 Guided Reading and Review
The Great Depression and World War II

A. As You Read

Directions: As you read Section 3 in the textbook, fill in details about each decade in American life.

1920s: The Jazz Age

1.

1930s: The Great Depression

2.

1940s: World War II

3.

B. Reviewing Key Terms

Directions: Briefly define each term. Note whether it applies to the 1920s, 1930s, or 1940s.

4. flapper _____

5. jazz _____

6. margin buying _____

7. Social Security _____

8. Holocaust _____

9. deficit spending _____

EPILOGUE

Section 4 Guided Reading and Review

The Cold War and the Civil Rights Era

A. As You Read

Directions: As you read Section 4 in the textbook, fill in the missing causes and effects.

Causes	Effects
Soviet leaders indicated their intent to spread communism throughout the world.	1.
2.	The Marshall Plan allotted $12 billion to help Europe recover.
Communist Fidel Castro seized control of Cuba.	3.
4.	People fought for African American rights in the civil rights movement.
5.	The United Farm Workers gained better working conditions.
More and more American troops were sent to Vietnam.	6.

B. Reviewing Key Terms

Directions: Briefly explain each person's role in the Cold War/Civil Rights era.

7. Fidel Castro _____

8. John F. Kennedy _____

9. Rosa Parks _____

10. Martin Luther King, Jr. _____

11. Lyndon Johnson _____

12. César Chavez _____

EPILOGUE

 **Section 5 Guided Reading and Review**

Into the Future

A. As You Read

Directions: As you read Section 5 in the textbook, answer the following questions:

1. Why was Richard Nixon threatened with impeachment? _____

_____

2. What were the goals of the conservatives who supported Ronald Reagan? _____

_____

_____

3. What actions did Reagan take as president? _____

_____

4. What were some of Bill Clinton's presidential policies? _____

_____

5. How did the Cold War end? _____

_____

6. What are some of the new challenges facing the United States? _____

_____

B. Reviewing Key Terms

Directions: Briefly define each term.

7. Watergate affair _____

8. détente _____

9. North American Free Trade Agreement _____